THE COMPLETE IDIOT'S GUIDE® TO

Rumi
Meditations

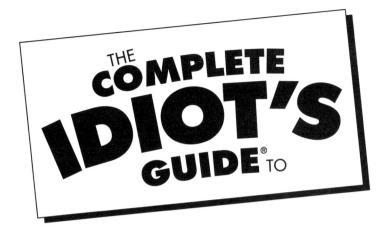

Rumi
Meditations

by Yahiya Emerick

ALPHA

A member of Penguin Group (USA) Inc.

ALPHA BOOKS

Published by the Penguin Group

Penguin Group (USA) Inc., 375 Hudson Street, New York, New York 10014, USA

Penguin Group (Canada), 90 Eglinton Avenue East, Suite 700, Toronto, Ontario M4P 2Y3, Canada (a division of Pearson Penguin Canada Inc.)

Penguin Books Ltd., 80 Strand, London WC2R 0RL, England

Penguin Ireland, 25 St. Stephen's Green, Dublin 2, Ireland (a division of Penguin Books Ltd.)

Penguin Group (Australia), 250 Camberwell Road, Camberwell, Victoria 3124, Australia (a division of Pearson Australia Group Pty. Ltd.)

Penguin Books India Pvt. Ltd., 11 Community Centre, Panchsheel Park, New Delhi—110 017, India

Penguin Group (NZ), 67 Apollo Drive, Rosedale, North Shore, Auckland 1311, New Zealand (a division of Pearson New Zealand Ltd.)

Penguin Books (South Africa) (Pty.) Ltd., 24 Sturdee Avenue, Rosebank, Johannesburg 2196, South Africa

Penguin Books Ltd., Registered Offices: 80 Strand, London WC2R 0RL, England

Copyright © 2008 by Yahiya (J. A.) Emerick

All rights reserved. No part of this book shall be reproduced, stored in a retrieval system, or transmitted by any means, electronic, mechanical, photocopying, recording, or otherwise, without written permission from the publisher. No patent liability is assumed with respect to the use of the information contained herein. Although every precaution has been taken in the preparation of this book, the publisher and author assume no responsibility for errors or omissions. Neither is any liability assumed for damages resulting from the use of information contained herein. For information, address Alpha Books, 800 East 96th Street, Indianapolis, IN 46240.

THE COMPLETE IDIOT'S GUIDE TO and Design are registered trademarks of Penguin Group (USA) Inc.

International Standard Book Number: 978-1-59257-736-1
Library of Congress Catalog Card Number: 2007935866

10 09 08   8 7 6 5 4 3 2 1

Interpretation of the printing code: The rightmost number of the first series of numbers is the year of the book's printing; the rightmost number of the second series of numbers is the number of the book's printing. For example, a printing code of 08-1 shows that the first printing occurred in 2008.

Printed in the United States of America

Note: This publication contains the opinions and ideas of its author. It is intended to provide helpful and informative material on the subject matter covered. It is sold with the understanding that the author and publisher are not engaged in rendering professional services in the book. If the reader requires personal assistance or advice, a competent professional should be consulted.

The author and publisher specifically disclaim any responsibility for any liability, loss, or risk, personal or otherwise, which is incurred as a consequence, directly or indirectly, of the use and application of any of the contents of this book.

Most Alpha books are available at special quantity discounts for bulk purchases for sales promotions, premiums, fund-raising, or educational use. Special books, or book excerpts, can also be created to fit specific needs.

For details, write: Special Markets, Alpha Books, 375 Hudson Street, New York, NY 10014.

Publisher: *Marie Butler-Knight*
Editorial Director: *Mike Sanders*
Managing Editor: *Billy Fields*
Executive Editor: *Randy Ladenheim-Gil*
Development Editor: *Susan Zingraf*
Senior Production Editor: *Janette Lynn*

Copy Editor: *Janet K. Zoya*
Cover Designer: *Kurt Owens*
Book Designer: *Trina Wurst*
Indexer: *Brad Herriman*
Layout: *Ayanna Lacey*
Proofreader: *Aaron Black*

Contents at a Glance

Contents

Introduction

Poetry has been one of the most common vehicles for expressing wisdom and cultural knowledge throughout human history. When words are strung together like pearls on a golden chain of rhyme and rhythm, they float much more easily into the heart and mind than mere lecturing. Moreover, when a weighty message is carried on the gentle stream of a poem, it's unthreatening, easy to remember, and a delight to hear. We are, in fact, creatures attuned to poetry!

Some of the greatest religious works of antiquity, such as the Psalms, the Qur'an, the Tao Te Ching, and others, use poetry to get their message across. When religion and poetry get married, the children can turn out to be truly beautiful! Now think of some of the best-loved stories that have survived through the ages, compositions as diverse as Homer's *Odyssey* or the *Canterbury Tales.* They were poetic in form and held a wide audience enthralled to their tales. Emily Dickenson, Robert Frost, and even some modern songwriters have the same effect on us today. Poetry as an art form seems to bring light for its own sake into our otherwise ordinary existence!

From the East, too, there has come a large number of poetic works that have stood the test of time. The works of Fariduddin 'Attar, Hafiz, Ibn 'Arabi, Jami', and Nizami stand out as classics in both their own languages and in English. There is another poet, however, whose work has towered above all others in both its appeal and widespread use, and that is the work of the thirteenth-century poet-master, Jalaluddin Rumi. Far from being merely pleasant selections to while away an afternoon with, his writings have shaped the thinking of generations of Muslims, both Sufi and orthodox, and his couplets are still taught in most schools throughout the Muslim world today.

Rumi was no austere theologian issuing edicts of doom in mere poetic form, however, for he had a different mission. His life and example was dedicated to becoming the living, breathing embodiment of what a conscientious and thoughtful Muslim should be. That he was a religious and faithful Muslim is never questioned, for he was an Imam, a religious lawyer and a teacher. Yet he was part of a tradition, handed down from generations before him, which saw in the Qur'an and the life of Prophet Muhammad the door that led the sincere seeker to the very threshold of Divine Love and light. For Rumi, his religion was the key to opening the doors to self-realization and ultimately absorption into the light of God.

This book you have in your hands is a compilation of some of Rumi's poems with accompanying meditations. Although I am not a disciple of Rumi, I have always enjoyed his expansive insight and wisdom, and I believe his words speak to all people regardless of who they are or where they come from. I hope that you enjoy these selections, and it's my sincere desire that Rumi can become a stepping-stone for you to explore the inner mysteries that make up the human heart. If one soul breathes easier because of what I have done here, then perhaps the faint breeze of such a sigh of relief may blow my way and make me smile for no reason. It might even reach Rumi, as well.

How This Book Is Organized

This book has been divided into four separate sections that group together Rumi's poems by theme.

Part 1, "Meet the Master," introduces who Rumi was and what forces shaped his life. We learn about his background, his illustrious father, his many travels, the people he met who influenced him, and the journey toward enlightenment he undertook seemingly by accident. His major works are introduced, and they set the stage for delving into the self-awareness journey.

Part 2, "Nothing for Something Is Everything," introduces the idea that people suffer from a lack of self-awareness. The drudgery and toil of our daily lives make us forget to take care of the most important person in our lives: ourselves. Rumi provides a path for remembering who we are and for identifying the essentials of awakening the sleeping mind.

Part 3, "Love and the Single Mind," explores what true love is and how to achieve it. When the light of Divine Love is awakened within us, our capacity for earthly love is ignited to the benefit of all around us.

Part 4, "In the Garden of Eternal Delight," presents some of Rumi's more memorable tales of wisdom and insight. Through animal fables, teaching stories, and practical applications of life skills, we learn how to apply the wisdom of Rumi to our own lives.

Extras

To help your learning experience be even more enjoyable and insightful, you'll find many of the following sidebars, including interesting tidbits of information, sprinkled liberally throughout the text.

Rumi's References

Throughout Rumi's works, he draws liberally on verses from the Qur'an, sayings of Muhammad, prominent scholars, and fellow poets through the centuries. These references are identified here.

Wisdom of the Ages

Here you will find the words of poets who have influenced Rumi in the development of his understanding. You will also find some of Rumi's own words here, as well.

Footprints of the Master

A treasure trove of useful information and background notes to help you understand Rumi's life and works in a better light.

def•i•ni•tion

This resource will provide you with translations of frequently used words and important terms related to the life of Rumi.

Acknowledgments

I really want to thank the people who made this book possible. This is my second *Complete Idiot's Guide* and the support I've received has been overwhelming. To Jacky Sach, my literary agent, I extend my gratitude for encouragement and helpful feedback. A special thank-you for Randy Ladenheim-Gil, my company guide, for all the kind assistance she extended in the completion of this manuscript. The staff at Alpha Books, a division of Penguin, has also been exceptional. My editors, Susan Zingraf, Janette Lynn, and Janet K. Zoya, deserve kudos for the hard task of making sense of my endless files, and finally, and most importantly, I would like to thank my family for shouldering more than their fair share of life's responsibilities during my time working on this book.

Trademarks

All terms mentioned in this book that are known to be or are suspected of being trademarks or service marks have been appropriately capitalized. Alpha Books and Penguin Group (USA) Inc. cannot attest to the accuracy of this information. Use of a term in this book should not be regarded as affecting the validity of any trademark or service mark.

Part 1

Meet the Master

Jalaluddin Rumi was one of the most complex men to inhabit the Muslim Middle Ages. His complexity lay in his broad wisdom and many decades of deep study. In fact, he received the finest education his time could offer. Yet, in an opportune moment of inspiration, he broke free from the confines of knowledge and took flight on a spiritual awakening that led him to the doors of inner truth. His complexity then took on the robe of simplicity, enabling him to share deep insights and wisdom with one and all.

Such was Rumi's ability to make the deepest mysteries clear that he attracted students from all religions. He became so beloved a figure that those around him felt his absence when he was away from them; and when he passed away, his funeral was attended by Muslims, Christians, and Jews. This was the effect that Rumi's life of love and teaching had. In this part you will learn about who Rumi was, the society and culture he lived in, the role of historical events and religion in his life, what he wrote, and the principles he stood for. You'll be amazed at the colorful and interesting life he led and the marvels of genius he penned.

Who Was Rumi?

In This Chapter

- ◆ The background of the Islamic culture and significant events that shaped Rumi's life
- ◆ Rumi's family of educators and his life of study
- ◆ The pivotal influence of mystic Shamsuddin
- ◆ The main factors causing Rumi to take up the study of the soul

It can be honestly said that Jalaluddin Rumi was an exemplary icon of what a true internationalist should be. His emphasis on tolerance, personal integrity, generosity, cooperation, and yes, genuine love for all things is an example for all people everywhere to emulate. So much so, UNESCO, a division of the United Nations, declared the year 2007 as the "Year of Rumi." Now it may seem odd that an international organization representing a diverse array of cultures, races, and religions would promote the life and thought of a thirteenth century Muslim poet. Yet when we look at what he stood for, it's apparent he's a perfect fit.

Through his many writings, speeches, and poems, Rumi embodied the spirit of the evolved human being: someone whom all could trust to be fair and attentive, to be patient and open-minded, and to be ever the beacon of enlightened toleration for all. In fact, Rumi counted among his students people of many different religions and backgrounds, who all saw within his teachings the best of what their own traditions had to offer.

In this book, we will explore the depth of Rumi—the man, his work, and its legacy—and the beauty of his teachings on love, peace, and enlightenment. Yet, who was Rumi? Where did he come from, and how did he gain such an expansive view of the human soul?

To begin our journey, let's head back in time and set the stage of the ancient Islamic world, learn about the events leading up to and during Rumi's life, and see what forces shaped the man of whom the United Nations said, "This is his year."

Setting the Stage

Our journey to Rumi begins 800 years ago, in the late twelfth and early thirteenth centuries, on the frontiers of the Islamic world. It stretched from western Africa and Spain all the way eastward through the wilds of central Asia and down into the spice islands of the Malay Archipelago, in present-day Malaysia. It was a fabled time and place straight out of the *Arabian Nights*, whose tales so captivated the West with images of flying carpets, fanciful bandits, mysterious nomads, and exotic locations. Of course, there weren't actually flying carpets, but this world at the time certainly exuded an exotic flair compared to that of the West, which only added to its intrigue.

> **Footprints of the Master**
>
> In the thirteenth century, medieval Baghdad was the most civilized city in the world. It boasted hundreds of libraries, free hospitals and colleges, as well as vast markets where the goods of both East and West could be had. In Europe, Baghdad was called "The Jewel of the World."

On the political front, Baghdad was the jewel of the Islamic world at this time, and the once proud caliphs (or leaders) of the waning 'Abbasid dynasty, a family of rulers who claimed descent from the Prophet's uncle, was nearing the end of its power as a motley host of newly Islamized Turks vied for real power behind the throne. Farther east into Persia, in the region known today as Turkey, local governors had already declared their independence from this central government and set up their own small fiefdoms, paying mere lip service to the symbol of Islamic unity in Baghdad.

Though the political structure of the Islamic world was fragmenting rapidly at this time, the cultural unity of the society of believers was still very much alive and well. *Muslims* of all types—merchants, scholars, pilgrims, adventurers, and rogues—could pass freely from one end of the Islamic world to the other and scarcely recognize any signs that the political boundaries had changed along the way. Indeed, the tradition of the wanderer was well ingrained in the psyche of the Muslim mind. So much so, the Prophet Muhammad once remarked, "How unfortunate for the person who dies close to home." This was the kind of world that Rumi's ancestors lived in, and it would be indicative of the course that Rumi's own life would take.

def·i·ni·tion

Muslims are those who believe in and practice the religion of Islam, which is the second-largest religion in the world today and is based on the teachings of Muhammad, who lived during the seventh century.

Rumi's Scholarly Lineage

On the northeast fringes of this Islamic society lay the small city of Balkh, located in present-day Afghanistan. It was a hardscrabble settlement nestled among the rugged foothills of the Hindu Kush mountains, truly a frontier town in every sense of the word. It was at the western end of a broad swath of Islamic territory that extended deep into central Asia. Islam had come to this region in the ninth and tenth centuries; yet, like typical attempts at civilizing outlying lands, the existing culture here was tempered by its essential free spirit and restless energy. In other words, they primarily marched to the beat of their own drum, so to speak.

Local rulers here, however, in attempts to legitimize their own power, often supported things having to do with the Islam religion even if they didn't always follow its dictates themselves. They erected *mosques*, built comfort stations for merchants on the fabled Silk Road (the trade route that ran from China to Europe), and sought out wandering scholars to sponsor in their backwater settlements of stone huts, bazaars, and rickety palaces. Religious books were also highly prized, which allowed for a steady flow of Islamic flavor to continually rain down over this exotic and untamed region.

> **def•i•ni•tion**
>
> A **mosque** is a building in which Muslims worship.

In the district of Balkh, there lived a well-known religious scholar named Ahmad al-Khatibi. His interest in scholarly studies led him to amass a large library of books and gain a reputation as a local judge. On this account, learning and scholarship became an ingrained occupation among his descendants. Al-Khatibi passed his love of knowledge on to his son, *Jalaluddin* Hussein. In turn, Hussein had the responsibility of instilling the same love of books in his own son, Baha'uddin Muhammad Walad, Rumi's father, who was born in 1152. However, Hussein never had the chance to educate his son due to his own premature death just two years after Baha'uddin was born. Therefore it was up to Hussein's widow (Baha'uddin's mother) named Mu'mina Khatun, who was a princess in the local emirate of Balkh, and his own father (al-Khatibi, Baha'uddin's grandfather), who lived to a ripe old age, to carry forth the scholarly tradition to young Baha'uddin.

> **def•i•ni•tion**
>
> The name *Jalaluddin* means "Glory of the Faith." Rumi was named after his grandfather Jalaluddin Hussein.

According to an anecdote handed down among the descendants of this family, when Hussein passed away, Baha'uddin's mother took the two-year-old boy by the hand and led him into his father's library. There she said to him, *"I was married to your father for the sake of these books. Your father studied these writings and thereby gained the spiritual mastery that made him famous throughout the Muslim world."* In time, under his grandfather's and mother's tutelage, Baha'uddin himself gained a reputation for learning and knowledge second to none.

Late in the year 1207, a son was born to Baha'uddin, and he knew what family legacy he would pass on to him. This son was named Jalaluddin Muhammad, later to be known as Rumi.

Baha'uddin Takes to the Road

Rumi was born in the town of Wakhsh, which lies just north of Balkh in present-day Tajikistan. At that time, Rumi's father Baha'uddin was a celebrated scholar in the region and a minor prince of the ruling emirate (or command.) Baha'uddin, however, removed himself from any political affairs to instead lead the life of a theologian and judge. His reputation for fairness and clarity of thought earned him a high reputation in the region. In fact, he had no peer locally except for the equally famous and erudite scholar Fakhruddin ar-Razi, whose works on religious doctrine earned him widespread fame. There are some indications, though, that the two men didn't particularly like each other given their different styles of thought—Baha'uddin was more spiritual by nature while Razi was more of a rationalist. Some writers have suggested that this was the cause for Baha'uddin's eventual self-imposed exile from this region, which he began in 1212.

Another probable reason for Baha'uddin's migration from Wakhsh lies in the rough-and-tumble nature of that volatile region, which straddled the worlds of both East and West. There had recently been uncertainty and turmoil in the local government, with the last overlord sultan of the Ghorid Dynasty having been killed in battle. In addition, the expanding ambitions of Ala'uddin Muhammad II—also known as Khwarizm Shah, a Turkish warlord from the south—led to an invasion and the siege of Balkh itself. Thus, when Rumi was about five years old, his father removed his family and settled them in the northern fortress town of Samarkand (in present-day Uzbekistan) to escape all of this unrest.

After Khwarizm Shah completed his conquests in Balkh and turned the eye of his interests elsewhere and things seemed more settled, Baha'uddin returned his family to the district of greater Balkh for a time.

Outrunning the Mongols

As a boy, Rumi received a classical Islamic education from his father, which included theology, law, and the Arabic language. His father's top student, Syed Burhanuddin Mohhaqiq, also tutored him. If nothing else had intervened in Rumi's world, he might have merely succeeded his father as a local luminary and his name may have been lost to history. Yet, history has a way of making the unexpected happen, and events beyond the control of any mortal were soon to send Rumi and his family on a journey taking them thousands of miles away.

Enter Khwarizm Shah once more. In the year 1218, when Rumi was 11 years old, the up-and-coming Mongol warlord named *Genghis Khan* sent emissaries to the Persian court in Balkh seeking trade deals and mutual recognition. Meanwhile, Khwarizm Shah had recently been thwarted in his efforts to take over the 'Abbasid Caliphate of Baghdad. Scholars believe Khawrizm Shah took out his frustrations on what he must have deemed to be the representatives of a pathetic nomadic chieftain—Genghis Kahn. Khwarizm Shah had these Mongol ambassadors beheaded and sent their remains back to the Great Khan, taking care to show as much disrespect as possible.

Footprints of the Master

Genghis Khan was a Mongol warlord who created one of the largest empires in world history. His forces conquered much of the known world from northern China to the borders of Europe. His forces devastated much of the Muslim world in the early thirteenth century, causing him to boast that he was the very punishment of God Himself sent upon the Muslims and Christians of the world.

The vengeance of Genghis Khan, produced from this one rash act of an arrogant ruler, was swift and terrible, with destruction of historic proportions. It unleashed a war machine, which eventually reached into Europe itself after causing the destruction of nearly half the Muslim world in the process. His army of 200,000 men swept down upon central Asia, burning every city to the ground, and torturing and killing practically every human being they came across in their mad fury. Any vestige of civilization was literally razed to the ground for thousands of square miles with millions of people killed, making these

Mongols history's first great genocidal horde. The Muslim world still has not fully recovered from this destruction, which destroyed half of its centers of learning and culture a mere eight centuries ago. By the year 1219, the situation in Balkh was looking ever more grim as the cruel Mongols inched closer. Baha'uddin himself made a prediction to the local governor that the city was doomed. He then took his family and headed southwestward toward the safer regions of the Muslim heartland.

A year later, the Mongols destroyed Balkh. In fact, the imminent threat of Mongol invasion would be a constant in Rumi's life, even on up into his later years. The land he had settled down in came under Mongol sway through political usurpation. Interestingly enough, Rumi never expressed outright hatred of this foe, and it was partly due to his gentle philosophy that the great grandchildren of the Mongols accepted Islam.

Rumi Sees the World

Rumi was fast approaching his teenage years when his father moved their family southwestward from the district of Balkh. The first stop they made was in the famous Persian city of Nishapur, located in present-day Iran. It was here that the young Rumi met the celebrated writer, Fariduddin 'Attar. 'Attar's philosophically and spiritually oriented works were widely known, especially his monumental epic, *The Conference of Birds*. 'Attar, it seems, was impressed with the lucidity and insight of Rumi, despite his youth, and 'Attar personally gave Rumi a copy of his mystical tract, *The Book of Secrets*. In fact, scholars today are of the opinion that 'Attar was one of the two great influences upon Rumi's thinking. (The other is thought to be the mystical Afghani poet and scholar, Hakim Sanai of Ghazni, who passed away some 60 years before Rumi was born.)

Baha'uddin was not planning to settle in Nishapur, however, for his aim seemed to lie elsewhere. In addition, the Mongols were not far behind in their relentless march into the heart of Persia. Fortuitously, Baha'uddin felt the urge to visit the holy city of Mecca in Arabia (present-day Saudi Arabia), and thus, Baha'uddin packed up his family and left Nishapur heading farther southwestward to Mecca. It was just in time, it seems, for shortly afterward the Mongols captured and destroyed Nishapur, killing up to 1,000,000 people in the process.

Footprints of the Master _____

Baha'uddin Walad was more than just a famous religious scholar. He was also a mystic philosopher with a large though discreet following. Some years before he passed away, Baha'uddin gave his son a copy of a book of his thoughts that he had written, entitled, *Ma'arif*, or *That Which Is Thought About*. A modern English translation of selections from this book by Coleman Barks and John Moyne is titled, *The Drowned Book*.

Given the times, it was expected that a person on any long journey through the heartland of Islam would make visits to the greatest cities. Accordingly, the itinerant family of Baha'uddin enjoyed sojourns in the fabled cities of Baghdad and eastern Syria. From there the family finally made their pilgrimage to Mecca. Then, after completing the holy rituals, they started on a long, meandering journey northward back through Syria until they finally reached Anatolia (the Asian side of present-day Turkey), the domain of the Seljuk tribe of Turks whose kingdom consisted of land recently seized from the Byzantine Romans. (The Byzantine Empire, centered on Greece and Turkey, was all that was left of the original Roman Empire.)

Settling in a small town in Anatolia named Laranda, Rumi, who was by then about 21 years old, had already accomplished more than most young men could at that time. Not only had he escaped the maniacal horde of invaders who had destroyed his homeland, Rumi was fortunate enough to have also been fully trained in the classical arts and sciences. He traveled through the most important cities of Islam, had moved from his home to a land over 1,000 miles away, and had enjoyed the opportunity to meet with some of the most celebrated mystics and scholars of his time. His own father was one such man himself!

Going Back to School

Between the years 1222 and about 1227, Rumi lived quietly in Laranda. He continued his studies with his father, and most likely worked as a teacher of some sort. Sometime in these years, he married a young woman named Ghevher (Jawhar) Khatun, who herself was a transplanted resident of Balkh. She soon bore him a son, whom Rumi affectionately named Sultan Walad (after his father). It was also during this time that Rumi's brother Ala'uddin passed away, and when Rumi's second child was born about two years later, he named him Ala'uddin in honor of his deceased sibling.

Unexpectedly, in the year 1228, Rumi's father Baha'uddin received an invitation from the enlightened Seljuk Sultan named Ala'uddin Kayqubad to head a religious academy in the nearby city of Konya (formerly known as Iconium). Baha'uddin accepted the offer and moved his family there, to what would become their final home. Baha'uddin, however, passed away in 1231 after only two and a half years at the head of his academy. The logical choice for a replacement headmaster was, of course, his learned son Rumi. Thus Jalaluddin Rumi took over the school, which produced a steady supply of religious and legal scholars for the Seljuk domain.

Footprints of the Master

Most cultures use occupations or place names as an extra device to identify someone's origins. The same holds true in Middle Eastern culture, where such details often became addendums to a person's full name. When Jalaluddin Muhammad lived in Balkh, his name was Jalaluddin Muhammad *al-Balkhi*. When he had settled in Anatolia, he gained the alternative name, Jalaluddin Muhammad *al-Rumi*. The Arabic term for the Romans is Rūm, and Anatolia had only recently been wrested from the Byzantine Romans.

This might have been the extent of Rumi's achievements, save for the intervention of fate. Busy as he was in his administrative and teaching duties, which were supplemented by regular stints as a preacher in the main mosque of Konya, Rumi lived the life of an unassuming religious and scholastic functionary. He took no real interest in composing written works himself, although he enjoyed reading the poetry of Sanai, 'Attar, and al-Mutanabbi, the last of whom was a celebrated (and colorful, to put it mildly) writer of a previous age. But soon Rumi's world would begin to change.

A Voice from the Past

One day, heaven opened a door for Rumi. One of his father's old students named Syed Burhanuddin showed up in Konya unannounced, and

Rumi eagerly took him as a teacher and mentor. Although Rumi had long known that his father leaned toward *mysticism* and esoteric spirituality, it wasn't until Burhanuddin revealed the full extent of his father's spiritual orientation that Rumi became intrigued with the idea of exploring the inner secrets of the soul.

def•i•ni•tion

Mysticism is the belief that personal communication or union with the divine is achieved through intuition, faith, introspective religious practice, or sudden insight as opposed to more traditional forms of public worship.

Between the years 1232 and 1236, Burhanuddin took over responsibility for supervision of the academy started by Rumi's father. He also tutored Rumi in the spiritual aspects of Islam and in the secret knowledge of self-actualization. He then sent Rumi to Syria for further training in the spiritual sciences with renowned teachers of the day. Rumi began to compose some elementary poetry in Arabic, and his range of literary skills increased exponentially. When Rumi finally returned to Konya in 1237, he had even more impressive credentials under his belt. It is said that to complete his training, Rumi spent three periods of forty days each in intense devotion, contemplation, and reflection. When this was accomplished, Burhanuddin declared Rumi a full adept of the Sufi Path and then he told him, "Go and decorate the souls of men with fresh life and unending mercy; revive all those lifeless bodies in this world with your love and thoughts." Thereafter, Rumi assumed the role of headmaster in the academy once more, and the aged Burhanuddin took his leave and moved to a nearby city in the year 1240, passing away two years later.

Rumi Meets the Mystic

Slowly, Rumi gained some fame for himself among the people of southeastern Anatolia. His academy attracted many students, and he seemed poised to follow in his father's footsteps as a renowned scholar and mystic. He also took to writing an ever-greater amount of poetry and prose, though mostly in Persian, which was considered the voice of the genteel class throughout the Muslim world.

He once remarked on his need to compose poetry in order to keep people's attention. Unlike his father back in Balkh, Rumi had no locally established reputation that would make people listen to him for his own sake. But as time passed, Rumi's compositions did earn him a loyal following and all seemed to go on as life might be expected for one who worked so hard. Then an unexpected meeting changed Rumi's life forever.

The story is told in slightly differing versions, but the basic outline is as follows. In October of 1244, Rumi was returning to his home from the academy, accompanied by some of his students. Along the way, he happened to pass through a market. Suddenly, a bedraggled-looking stranger approached him and urgently asked him, "Leader of the Muslims, who was greater, the Prophet, or Bayazid Bustami?" Now this was an odd question, for Bustami was a poet and religious mystic of the ninth century, while the Prophet Muhammad was, well, *the Prophet!*

Rumi's References

Bayazid Bustami (d. 874 C.E.) was a Persian mystic who was among the earliest Sufi masters. He was also the first to speak of the Sufi concept of annihilation in God (*fana fillah*), an idea similar to the Eastern concept of nirvana. He is quoted as saying, "I stood with the pious and I found no progress with them. I stood with the warriors in the cause (of God) and I found not a single step of progress with them. Then I said, 'O God, what is the way to You?' and God said, 'Abandon yourself and come to Me alone.'"

Rumi later described his initial reaction to this seemingly blasphemous inquiry this way: "Because of the enormity of that question, it seemed as if the seven heavens were ripped to shreds and crashed down upon the earth. Great turmoil churned within my soul and set my thoughts on fire, from which I imagined a pillar of smoke rising all the way up to the throne of God." Rumi then answered the stranger, whose unkempt appearance was indicative of a wandering *dervish*, by stating, "The Prophet is the greatest among men, so why do you speak of Bayazid?"

def•i•ni•tion

A **dervish** is a wandering mystic of the Middle East.

The stranger then exclaimed, "So why did the Prophet say, 'We don't know You, (O God), as You should be known,' while Bayazid said, 'I am glorified! I am great! I am the powerful one'?"

Rumi understood. The man was trying to get across the idea that Bayazid had hit upon some secret knowledge of God that made him feel at one with the Divine. The Prophet, however, was continually beseeching God for more favor in his desire to know God on a deeper level, possibly revealing a deficiency in his exposure to God's full reality. Therefore, Rumi offered an explanation for Bayazid's strange utterance by saying, "Bayazid's thirst (for God) was quenched in just one gulp. He spoke of being full, but the jug of his (limited) understanding was what was filled up. The light he received was only as much as the light that comes in through the skylight of a house. The Prophet, on the other hand, wanted to receive more to drink, and his (relentless) thirst remained unquenched (due to the expansive nature of his heart) … He spoke of being thirsty, for he always asked to be brought closer (to God)."

The force of this logic stunned the dervish, whose name was Shamsuddin of Tabriz. He let loose a yelp of surprise and then fainted. Rumi took pity on him and asked his students to carry the unconscious man back to the academy. When Shamsuddin awoke, he approached Rumi and placed his head on his knees in respect. Thereafter, Rumi took him as his special confidant and companion.

Soon after Shamsuddin entered Rumi's life, Rumi began to neglect his family and students. He preferred to spend most of his waking hours in deep conversation with the wanderer who had literally come into his life out of nowhere.

Rumi's Soul Takes Flight

Rumi spent the next three months in the exclusive company of the mysterious dervish, Shamsuddin of Tabriz. Rumi's family became alarmed at this, even as his students began to grow ever more jealous, having their studies interrupted as they were. What did the two friends talk about? What secret knowledge did they discover? Rumi alludes to the substance of their spiritual discourse in his later collection of thoughtful poems known as the *Divan* or *Discourses*. They spoke of God, of

Divine truth, of knowing the self, and of realizing the liberation of the soul while still physically bound by earthly shackles. After a lifetime of studying with so many masters of the soul, Rumi finally felt that he had found in Shamsuddin a perfect mirror to his own restless spirit.

Meanwhile, the students of the academy grew increasingly irked by the loss of their master to this mystic. Apparently, Shamsuddin felt the daggers of their constant animosity, and as suddenly as he had appeared in Rumi's life, he disappeared without a trace. Rumi was devastated, and began to lament his loss in verse. He started to compose ecstatic odes to his friendship with Shamsuddin and withdrew from society for a time. He also developed the habit of slowly turning in circles as he praised God, and this is the origin of the "whirling" that his later followers transformed into a highly stylized ritual form of meditation.

Rumi's References

Why did Rumi begin to rotate slowly as he meditated upon God? Perhaps it was due to the influence of the Qur'an, which contains this verse: "To God belongs the East and the West; wherever you turn is His Presence. He is the All-Pervading, the Observant." (2:115) This verse is also recited by devotees of Rumi at the close of ceremonies marking his passing from the world. This commemoration of his death occurs on December 17 each year all over the world.

Eventually, about two years after disappearing, Shamsuddin turned up in the southern city of Damascus, Syria. When Rumi learned of his reappearance, he dispatched his faithful elder son, Sultan Walad, to retrieve him. This time, Rumi sought to ensconce Shamsuddin by marrying him off to a woman who lived in his extended household. Upon doing so and for the next two years, Rumi reveled again in the company of his spiritual soul mate. Yet, jealousy from the family and students reared its ugly head once more, and in the year 1248, Shamsuddin disappeared again, forever. Suspicion of foul play quickly fell upon Rumi's younger son, Ala'uddin, who seemed to be at the head of a conspiracy among Rumi's disgruntled students. Though no definitive evidence ever came to light to prove such a link, Rumi must have had his own suspicions, for when Ala'uddin passed away a little over a decade later, Rumi didn't attend the funeral.

Composition of the *Divan*

After the final disappearance of Shamsuddin, Rumi was consumed by
an extended period of soul-searching. He continued to compose poems
and odes to assuage his wounded heart, and this ever-growing body
of work formed the basis of his book, *Divan*, which he dedicated to
the memory of Shamsuddin of Tabriz. These beautiful and emotional
poems spoke of a platonic form of love between a student and his lost
master. Here is some of what he wrote in his musings:

> I never used to be like this. I was never senseless nor bewildered.

> There was a time when I was wise like you, not crazy, insane, or
> broken like I am now.

> I wasn't someone who loved life without form or substance.

> I used to ask, "Who's this? What's that?" Endlessly, I used to seek
> out the answers.

> You're endowed with wisdom, so sit a while and ponder how I
> could have been like that before.

> Perhaps, I haven't changed all that much. I used to work hard to
> be better than everyone else, but I was never pursued by expansive
> love before.

> I tried to rise above the very sky itself with the strength of my
> ambition; yet, I didn't know the truth. In reality, I was just wander-
> ing about in the desert. In the end, I dug a treasure from out of
> the ground.

> From the *Divan*

Rumi Realizes the Greater Truth

In time, Rumi realized the brunt of his dilemma: he was lament-
ing the loss of his friend and confidant, when in reality he needed to
turn inward even more deeply to satisfy the real longing of his soul.
He needed to look for God's light within his heart, and not depend
so much on the presence of another. To do that, he realized, he had
to learn how to free his heart from all self-imposed limitations and

worldly attachments. Thus, his quest for inner-liberation accelerated in earnest.

Around the year 1250, Rumi met an old student of a former teacher. This man, whose name was Salahuddin Zarkub, was a humble goldsmith, unschooled in the traditional sense, yet he had an expansive frame of mind and he provided Rumi with a sounding board for his ideas.

The story is told that one day Rumi was walking in town when he was suddenly attracted to the sounds of hammering coming from Zarkub's gold shop. This gave Rumi a flash of inspiration and he began to praise God while rotating slowly in the street. When Zarkub saw the religious scholar outside his shop turning in circles, he ordered his workers to keep beating on the gold for as long as the scholar continued his moving meditation. Then Zarqub ran outside and joined Rumi and his students in their ritual, which lasted half the day. Afterward, Zarqub dedicated himself to Rumi and became his close friend. Perhaps mindful of what had befallen his other friend, Shamsuddin, when he had clung too closely to him, Rumi carried on a more muted friendship with Zarkub—yet he did marry his son Sultan to Zarqub's daughter Fatimah!

A few years later, Rumi's wife Ghevher passed away. After mourning her loss for a time, he eventually remarried. His new wife, a former Christian named Kira, bore him three children: two boys and a girl. Rumi's reputation for insight and his fame also grew throughout the region and beyond, and his academy attracted an ever more diversified student body. In fact, curious Christians and Jews began to attend his lectures regularly, and he welcomed all seekers of knowledge with open arms.

The Writing of the *Mathnawi*

Some time between the years 1259 and 1260, Rumi's top student, Husamuddin Chelebi, asked his master to leave a record of his teachings for posterity. As the story goes, Rumi pulled a page of 18 verses out of his turban to signal he had already begun thinking in that direction. For the next several years, Rumi dictated his epic collection of poetry, *Mathnawi*, or *Rhymed Couplets*, as Husamuddin recorded them. At the completion of each volume, out of a composition that would

def•i•ni•tion_____

The term *mathnawi* means rhymed verses or couplets.

eventually span six large books, Rumi would listen to Husamuddin as he read the poems back to him, and would revise them as needed. When it was completed, the *Mathnawi* would consist of over 25,000 verses.

This composition, which drew heavily upon the teachings of the Qur'an, the sayings of Muhammad, and the stories of the prophets and saints of the past, resembled something of a commentary on the nature of spirituality in the Islamic religion. (The *Mathnawi* was even called "the interpretation of the Qur'an in Persian," by the famous classical poet Jami'.) It was of such sublime quality in its insights and literary techniques that it achieved nearly instantaneous fame among the educated circles of the day. Rumi's verses would come to influence Muslim thought and culture ever afterward, and his works are still read throughout the Muslim world today, even as they've found a home in the West, as well. Rumi himself advised people on how they should approach his *Mathnawi* in these words:

> Every shop sells something different. The *Mathnawi* is the shop for (spiritual) destitution, my child.
>
> In the cobbler's shop, there's fine leather; any wood you see there is only for molding shoes.
>
> Tailors have silk and yellow-colored cloth (in their shops); any iron there is only for use as a measure.
>
> Our *Mathnawi* is the shop for unity (with the divine); anything you see there besides the One (God) is just an idol!
>
> *Mathnawi* VI, 1525 –1528

def•i•ni•tion_____

The term for an Islamic mystic is a **Sufi.** The word means "wool" in Arabic, and it describes the coarse woolen clothes that Sufis often wore to remind them that this world was not a place in which to find meaningful comfort.

In other words, the *Mathnawi* points people toward the Divine presence of a loving God. If anyone tries to read into it other than what it was designed to be, then it is not what the author intended. (Indeed, Rumi represented an orthodox position in the main, and his practice of *Sufi* mysticism was by no means a major cause for derision among conservatives in classical Islamic civilization, especially since such practices were often a part of the standard religious curriculum of study in those days!) When Rumi completed his dictation of the *Mathnawi*, he had every reason to believe it would be accepted from one end of the Muslim world to the other—and it was.

Rumi is buried in a mausoleum in Konya, Turkey, next to the Selimye Mosque.

Footprints of the Master

When Rumi had fallen ill during the final year of his life, he never prayed for healing. His wife Kira once remarked to those around him, "He needs at least three or four hundred years of life so he can fill the world with inner truths and answers." Rumi heard what she said, and he replied thusly, "Why is that? Why is that? We're neither Pharaoh nor Nimrod. What have we got to do with this world of dirt? How can we have peace and eternity here? We're imprisoned in this dungeon so that a few prisoners can be set free. We hope that we'll return to God's beloved (prophet) very soon."

As he neared the twilight of his golden years, Rumi spent more time in meditation, prayer, and writing. He appointed Husamuddin to head his academy, and then he receded from active involvement in the mundane affairs of the world. In the winter of 1273, Rumi fell ill. Doctors of every religion attended to him, unable to diagnose his ailment. Among his parting words to his students, he said, "I have two things I'm attached to in this world; one of them is the body, and the other is all of you. When, by God's mercy, I am removed from the world of loneliness and distraction, my attachment to you will yet remain." He passed away in mid-December of the same year and was laid to rest in his adopted home of Konya. Today, a beautiful shrine adorns the site of his grave. It's a solemn place visited by thousands of tourists and spiritual wanderers every year.

Now that you have an understanding of who Rumi was, where he came from, and the culture and times he lived in, in the next chapter we'll explore Rumi's methodology for achieving spiritual satisfaction. This is the lasting legacy of a man whose life and work have earned him the admiration of the world.

The Least You Need to Know

◆ Rumi grew up during violent wartime in the Middle East, and his family was moved several times by his father to escape harm.

◆ Rumi came from a scholarly family with his own father being a prominent spiritualist.

◆ Rotating slowly in circles is a spiritual meditation style that Rumi began and is known for.

◆ Shamsuddin was a mystic who Rumi met by chance and who had a profound spiritual effect on him.

◆ Through his studies and life experiences, Rumi became an expert in understanding the human heart and soul, and established a large following. He taught people how to find meaning in their lives.

Chapter 2

Rumi and His Worldview

In This Chapter

- Learning what the basis of Rumi's philosophy was regarding the soul and our ultimate fate

- Discovering Rumi's belief in our angelic and animal sides and which we should seek to cultivate and why

- Exploring how to recognize the hidden depth of your own heart and how to coax it out of hiding

- Understanding what Rumi means when he asks you to become drunk with divine love

When people think of Rumi, especially after the great proliferation of "Rumi books" that have appeared in the Western world of late, they often conjure images of a happy sort of fellow who loved everyone and never judged. In this, he joins the ranks of Buddha and Jesus in the multicultural pantheon of noble, nonjudgmental souls. While it is true that Rumi was a remarkably open-minded man in all respects, it must not be forgotten that he was more than just a poet of wit and insight. His words, his poems, served a purpose and were merely the vehicle by which he got his message across. So what was the foundation of his message? What did he base his philosophy on? These are essential questions that must be answered to better understand how his overall worldview permeates his every written thought.

In this chapter, we're going to take a look at Rumi's outlook on the basic nature and purpose of life, as well as take a deeper look into some of the dangers he identified that can hold a soul back from its true potential.

Rumi and His Religion

Rumi, as we learned in Chapter 1, was a deeply religious man. He believed without question in the existence of a supernatural presence Whom he knew as God or Allah. In Rumi's worldview, God is the primary source for the incredible depth and potential within the human soul, and God is the One with Whom all people should seek communion for their ultimate peace of mind. Also a devout and observant Muslim, Rumi considered the Qur'an to be the beacon that points the way toward union with God.

In the same spirit, all of Rumi's many writings are, by and large, extensions of the essential message of the best in the Islamic tradition. Mysticism was merely the stepping-stone he used in his exploration of the inner self. Indeed, it was through the lens of Islam—which is a remarkably tolerant and progressive faith, current hysteria and political conditions aside—that Rumi was able to realize that spirituality was universal. Whether a person was Muslim, Christian, Jewish, Buddhist, secular, or whatever, Rumi understood that we all have a soul from the same Source. He believed that everyone could unlock the door to attaining spiritual bliss, if they would only expand their vision and be willing to open themselves, with determination and patience, to their inner potential. Rumi wrote the following:

> Sometimes we're hidden, other times revealed;

> We're all Muslims, Christians, and Jews. No matter our race or creed, our hearts are formed the same; it's just that every day we see through a different mental frame.

> From the *Divan*

Contrary to what some admirers (and critics) of Rumi have said, he never denigrated or belittled the importance of Islam vis-à-vis other religions, nor did he ever renounce his faith in the teachings of Muhammad. The often-quoted line from some versions of

Rumi's References

The Qur'an formed the basis of Rumi's teachings on tolerance. He had memorized the entire Qur'an in his youth (a common Islamic practice).

the *Divan* in which he supposedly said, "I am not a Christian, a Jew, a Zoroastrian, or a Muslim," does not appear in any of the oldest manuscripts of that collection. And it was most probably, as modern scholars such as Reynold Nicholson suggest, a poem written by someone else and inserted in a later edition of the text for his own purposes.

Far from being a renegade to his religion, Rumi was an example of the best it could produce. In fact, he gained the rare and precious insight that only the most expansive minds ever discover, that the Truth, the Highest Truth, cannot be contained in a mere label. When there is Muslim, Christian, and Jew, there is one level of understanding. When there is complete submission to God, the significance of the label falls away and the inner sincerity of each individual becomes the arbiter of his or her true worth. This is the logical result of this line from the Qur'an: "Those who believe (in Islam) and those who are Jewish, Christian, or Sabian, whoever believes in God and the Last Day and who does what's morally right, their reward will be with their Lord, and they'll have no cause to fear nor regret." (2:62) Thus, Rumi saw beyond the shell of dogma and surface understandings. On this he wrote the following:

> Your perception is defined by how well you understand the world. Your impure senses are the curtain that prevents you from becoming pure.

> Wash your sense of perception for a while in the water of far-sightedness. Know that this is how Sufi's wash their cloaks! When you've become purified, the insight of the pure will tear away the curtain and attach itself to you.

> If the entire world was illuminated and filled with shapes, only the eye would ever notice that loveliness. Imagine if you closed your eye and turned your ear toward the flaxen hair of a lovely beauty.

The ear would protest (in its blindness), saying, "I cannot see any shapes at all. It's only when a shape makes a sound that can I respond. I can only practice what I'm skilled at, and my skill is only to hear sounds and words, nothing more."

Mathnawi IV, 2384–2390

With that said, while his overall doctrines remained within the basic parameters of medieval Islamic orthodoxy, at times Rumi did stretch those boundaries to provide new insights. This is one of the things that has made the study of Rumi's teachings so delicious for so many generations of spiritual seekers: they're fresh and at times delightfully unexpected. When you explore Rumi's philosophy regarding the nature of the human being more closely, you can begin to gain a deeper appreciation for why he was so passionate in his call for inner reform.

People Are the Richest Treasure

In Islamic philosophy, human beings are the most important of all of God's creations. No diamond or star or galaxy can match the human mind and all its capacity, and Rumi believed this wholeheartedly. He often echoed the verse of the Qur'an that says, "Human beings are the best of creation." (95:4) The basic idea in this position is that conscious thought trumps all other miraculous inventions. The apex of all creation, then, is the human spirit and mind. How can this be so? Well, no matter how spectacular a supernova may be, in the end it has no appreciation for how beautiful it is. No matter how gorgeous the sunrise, no snail, turtle, or crow composes poems to its suggestive splendor or is moved to inspiration by its endless possibilities in the imagination.

God can make many a wondrous thing, but consciousness is worth more than all the rocks in the universe! In this regard, there is a saying, attributed to Muhammad and cherished by generations of Sufis, that explains why God created human beings in the first place. According to this report, God Himself said, "I was a treasure whom no one knew; I wished to be known." Humanity's ability to think, to imagine, to reason, to appreciate, to believe, to deny, and yes, even to love for abstract reasons, sets us apart from all the rest of creation and makes us beloved of God. This is how Rumi puts it:

A single exhale from a human being is worth as much as a soul. A single hair that falls from him is worth more than a goldmine.

From the *Divan*

Wisdom of the Ages

Rumi wrote: "The Prophet said that God said, 'When I created (human beings) it was for a noble purpose. I created them with the expectation that they might gain something good from Me, and that they might get their hands wet with My blessed honey. I had no intention of taking anything from them, nor do I want to tear the coat off a naked (beggar).' During that short span of time since (God) drove my spirit from His presence, my eye has remained always fixated on His beautiful face."

Mathnawi II, 2635–2638

Human beings are the greatest show in town, on Earth, or anywhere else in the universe. Thus, by extension, our focus must not be centered only upon the mere objects and forms that surround us, for they're not the source or object of true beauty. For Rumi, the real treasure lies within. When a human being brushes off the dust shrouding his or her soul, a sparkling diamond of self-actualization and empowerment appears. This is the crux of our purpose, so to speak, as Rumi would concur when he wrote, "Humanity is the object of the universe."

Humans Are Not Born Sinful

Rumi approached the matter of human nature from the perspective of his religion. In Islamic theology, people are not born sinful. Instead, they're born basically neutral with a slight disposition toward good and an inner need to find meaning (by discovering their dependence upon and need for God). People can corrupt themselves at their core, however, if they let unchecked material desires get the better of their intellect and basic moral nature. According to Rumi, this path gradually deadens the soul, while the path to salvation lies within the proper use of the heart and mind.

The path we choose determines how open or closed our souls become to their true nature. Then, by extrapolation, it determines how tranquil or miserable we will be in our lives. That's why it's so essential, in Rumi's estimation, that we embark upon the process that leads us toward inner peace. We have nothing to lose except our shortcomings, and everything to gain by getting in touch with who we really are inside. He wrote the following:

> You're not only water (spirit), nor are you only soil (a physical being). You're something else entirely. You transcend the world of mud, for you're on a journey (toward self-realization).
>
> Your physical body is merely a conduit, while your soul is the eternal water that courses through it. You won't be aware of either, as long as you stay bottled up within yourself.
>
> From the *Divan*

Why So Many Seek God

The human predisposition to seek meaning in God deserves further explanation. According to Rumi's Muslim beliefs, every human being has some part of God's own spirit implanted within him or her before birth. This spirit "material" is not "God," but a substance made from the Divine Matter that is God. Think of taking a bucketful of water from the ocean. It's no longer the ocean, but it's still water. God put a soul or spirit, derived from His own matter, within each of us as a gift to help point the way back toward Him.

The idea is that our inner sense of separation will gently prompt us all our lives to seek to reunite with the universal expanse of God, so we can achieve tranquility of mind here and reunion with God "over there." In other words, we should realize that the bucket of water we're holding belongs back in the ocean! This is the crux of the entire Sufi philosophy of "union" or "annihilation" (*fana*) in God. To join our spiritual matter with the divine, while still being alive here in this world, helps us transcend the limits of the flesh and achieve a state of enlightenment. Rumi exhorts us to take up this quest in these words:

> Listen, O drop, give yourself up without regret, and in exchange, gain the Ocean.

Listen, O drop, take this honor upon yourself, and in the embrace of the Sea be safe from harm. Who could be so lucky?—an Ocean calling to a drop!

In God's name, in God's name, sell yourself and purchase (salvation) at once. Give a drop, and in return gain this Sea full of pearls.

Mathnawi IV, 2619–2622

Anyone who fails to take up this quest, who ignores the subtle promptings in his innermost being, and who lets his life be dictated by the fickle whims of his desires, merely becomes a slave to the material world, and like a worn-out car, will merely rust away long before his body has ceased to function.

Rumi's References

A cherished prophetic saying passed on by Sufis is: "God does not consider your looks or your bodies; rather He looks into your hearts and actions."

The Three Types of Being

It's human nature to wonder about our own inner selves. What kind of inner presence do we have? How are we different from the rest of creation? How can this knowledge help us to understand what we must do and the potential pitfalls we may have to face? These are important questions that lay the groundwork for our own conception of what our life journey will entail. Rumi identified three basic states of existence in the realm of living creatures. They are as follows:

- ◆ The transcendence of the angels.
- ◆ The animal or instinctual state.
- ◆ The dichotomy of humanity.

Starting with the angels, they are completely rational. They have no material concerns and know of no other reality than to be in complete awe and worship of the divine beauty of God. They're in a perfect state of unity.

The animal state, however, covers those creatures that are governed by instinct more than anything else. Such beings are slaves to their passions and physical needs. They give no thought to the ultimate end of their lives. They act without forethought, are driven by primitive emotions and prompts, and have no sense of their own transcendence or potential. Right and wrong mean little to them—there is only survival, protection of offspring, and individual gratification whenever possible.

The human being, on the other hand, has a little of the angel within him, and a little of the animal, as well. These two forces do battle on a daily basis. Those who lean more toward their angelic side become progressively more noble, self-aware, and moral, while those who incline toward the animal within themselves become more deluded by materialism, more a slave to their desires, and more likely to commit injustice and immorality with declining levels of remorse. Rumi describes the dichotomy of humanity like this:

> You're like a king, for as the verse says, "We have blessed the children of Adam." Thus, you travel both upon the dry land (of physical life) and upon the sea (of spiritual existence).

> You're part spirit, for as the verse says, "We carry them on the sea," so move beyond the line that says, "We carry them on the land."

> The angels have no way to walk upon the land (as physical beings), even as animals have no knowledge of the sea (of the spiritual realm).

> In your physical body, you're an animal, and in your spirit you're one of the angels, therefore you walk both upon the earth and within the heavens.

> Thus, a far-sighted person, who has had his heart inspired by God, still appears as an ordinary human. Though his material body is lying around here on the earth, yet his spirit is circling around in the sky.

Mathnawi II, 3773–3778

Wisdom of the Ages

Rumi once wrote: "There's a strange commotion above my head; birds are circling all around, particles are moving on their own. Is the One I love everywhere?"

From the *Divan*

Human beings must break free of their animalistic side and seek communion with their more noble side. This principle is not unique to Islamic theology, for most other religions contain similar exhortations, but Rumi made it a central focus of his philosophy. This process of awakening the soul is the only thing that can save us from misery in this life and perdition (everlasting punishment) in the afterlife, of which Rumi, as a practicing Muslim, believed. In Rumi's estimation, our physical bodies are merely rented vessels that we hold for a time before our souls escape, leaving empty shells behind. Will it be a soul that lived its life well and is worthy of eternal reward, or will it be sullied and wasted by a caretaker who didn't know how to use it? The choice is entirely up to us. Rumi wrote this:

> The body, like a mother, is pregnant with the spiritual child; death is the pain and stress of birth. All the souls that have passed over to the next life already are anxiously waiting to see in what state that proud spirit will be born.

Mathnawi I, 3514–3515

Love Is the Ultimate Goal

So we know why we're alive—to unlock our inner light and become worthy of God's greater light. We know what obstacles can hold us back—materialism and unchecked desires. We know that without embarking upon this quest for our soul, we run the risk of leading a bitter, unfulfilled life with little chance for meaningful happiness and spiritual relevance. So what is the great motivator in this endeavor, other than these fearful prospects? Is the path to self-actualization and inner peace merely defined by coercion and the threat of personal doom?

Of course not! While it's true that people avoid running into burning buildings as a matter of course, if a loved one is in there, no amount of fear ever enters the mind as we blindly rush into the flames for the object of our love. It's love and the ultimate meaning it provides that propel us forward in that case, and it's the same reason to begin our spiritual journey, as well. Love is the goal, and no amount of fear for any potential loss or pain should ever enter our minds after we've understood what we're so close to gaining. When we act upon our desire for love, we have no choice but to eventually become acquainted with the greatest love in the universe. Rumi said of this:

> One who loves seeks the object of his love with driving passion, so much so that when the beloved appears, the one who loved disappears (within the object of his desire).

> You are a lover of God, and God is of such a nature that when He comes, not even a single hair on your head will yet remain. A mere glance of His can make 100 of you vanish into thin air.

> I think you're in love with the empty (concerns of this world), yet you're just a shadow in love with the sun. When the (real) sun arrives, the shadow quickly disappears.

Mathnawi III, 4620–4623

For mystics of all religions, whether it be practitioners of Jewish Kabbalism, Christian Gnosticism, Muslim Sufism, Taoism, Buddhism, Hindu Vedanta, or even New Age spirituality, the essential principle of enlightenment is a love so absolute that it absorbs one's own soul in a mystical union with the Universal Way. This common thread of methods and goals further lends credence to Rumi's belief, derived from Islamic theology, that all true religions came from the same Source: God. As Rumi wrote, "Love's nationality is set apart from any religion. The religion and nationality of the lover is the Beloved. The lover's quest is separate from any other quest, for Love is the astrolabe that points to the mysteries of God."

Regardless of what you name the Source, love permeates all aspects of physical life, so much so that when injustice or violence occurs, the total absence of love in those instances is jarring, immediate, and unsettling. Love cannot stand the effects of unjustified hate and oppression. Those who struggle for justice to be restored are really struggling to bring love back into the lives of all those concerned. Can you think of a single noble figure from history who wasn't driven by love? The saying "Love conquers all" may be a cliché, yet without love, all are lost.

Islamic mystics, Rumi included, draw many examples of love from the sayings of prophet Muhammad. One of their favorites is the following. The Prophet said, "God divided His mercy into 100 parts, out of which He retains 99 parts with Him. He sent the one remaining portion to earth. From this one portion of love emanates all the compassion that the whole of creation shows toward each other, so much so that a mother animal will lift her hoof above her young lest it should get hurt." The love of the Divine is absolute love, and we are given only a tiny glimpse of it in our basic nature. The path of the mystically oriented person is to unlock the rest. Rumi commented upon this often. In one famous passage, he wrote this:

> Love is an endless sea, upon which the heavens are but a speck of foam. The revolving heavens are thus moved by waves of love. If it wasn't for (God's) love, then the earth would be frozen solid.
>
> How could lifeless soil turn into a plant (without His love)? How could plants sacrifice themselves (as food) and become (sentient beings) with a spirit? How could that spirit think to sacrifice itself (through self-denial) for the sake of that (Divine) Breath whose lightest touch made Mary pregnant (with her miracle-child)?
>
> (Without God's love) each of those things would be as solid and dense as ice; how could they ever flutter around like locusts in their endless search (for survival, meaning, and truth)?
>
> Every speck is in love with that Perfection, and each of them is rushing ever higher toward it like a sapling (reaching for the sun). Their haste betrays their real object, which is to say, "All glory to God!" They're cleansing their bodies for the sake of the spirit within.
>
> *Mathnawi* V, 3853–3859

Seek the Company of Lovers

Like attracts like, so they say, and love attracts those who are inclined toward love. If people want to open their hearts and let the light shine in their innermost being, they're really expressing a desire for love. At first it may seem like an ordinary, ill-defined "love" with a lowercase "l," but in time, when the initial taste of love leaves the person wanting more, she may realize that the Ultimate Love does, in fact, exist, and she may grasp for it with all her heart and soul. These are the people who are called "lovers" in mystical poetry. That Ultimate Love is then named "the Beloved."

Rumi believed that people who are on the same path should keep company with each other. He had many acolytes, confidants, and students of his own, both male and female, even as his father had. It's through the companionship of fellow seekers that insight is gained and success is accelerated. Thus, Rumi recorded many quatrains and exhortations to not only seek the aid of a spiritual Master in your quest, but also to seek the company of those who share a similar goal as yourself.

One of the books that influenced Rumi, *The Conference of the Birds*, mentioned in Chapter One, is a classic example of a group dynamic at work, leading to the ultimate success of all who had the will and patience to complete the journey. Here is what Rumi said on the importance of sharing the spiritual journey with others:

> The Prophet said, "God has declared, 'I am not found in places high or low, nor on the earth nor in the sky will you find (My Home). I am present in the hearts of My faithful servants; If you seek Me, then seek in these hearts.'"
>
> *Mathnawi* I, 2653–2655

The quest for enlightenment, however, doesn't require us to give up our lives, our jobs, our families, and our interests. It doesn't hold out the threat of snatching us away from what we cherish. There is no requirement to lead a life of quiet contemplation in the company of hermits. This is demonstrated amply in the cosmopolitan nature of Rumi's followers and students. They were drawn from all walks of life, all religions, and all classes. Some spent more time learning from the Master, while others attended his lectures and went back to their normal lives with a few useful lessons and insights they could put into practice. In your own life, you decide how much time you want to devote to awakening your inner spirit. We all move at a different pace and achieve results in our own time. Rumi wrote this:

> Your job is not to seek for love, but merely to identify all the barriers within yourself that you have built against it.
>
> From the *Divan*

If the desire is there, and the spiritual Master is found, sit with him or her as you are able—in person or in the privacy of your own home as you read his or her words. This book you hold in your hands contains several nuggets of wisdom left behind by one particularly skilled Master of the spirit. You may learn much from them, and you may progress beyond these and seek even deeper knowledge. Whatever your goal and whatever stage you choose to progress to, may it be easy upon you and may you smile one day when some lesson hits home. At that same moment, there may be others discovering the same as you. Rumi suggests, "So seek them out and share your experiences—you might benefit each other even more than you can imagine!"

Footprints of the Master

Islamic mystics trace their movement all the way back to the first generation of Muhammad's followers, some of whom were very inclined toward the inner qualities of faith and spirituality. By the time of classic Islamic civilization, Sufi brotherhoods, or *tariqas*, were well established all over the Muslim world from Spain to central Asia and deep into India and west Africa.

Drunk with Divine Love

According to Rumi (and the mystics of every faith), when a person completes his quest for enlightenment, he's in such perfect alignment with Universal Love that he literally sheds all earthly fears and lives for the day when his body finally expires, releasing his spirit into what he already has come to know (as much as is humanly possible). There is no longer any fear of death, no remorse for lost material gains, and no desire to commit any injustice to any living thing. His physical body has been tamed—it has to be—so he can rise above it and attain the most perfect spiritual state. Rumi whimsically commented on this when he said the following:

> Know that this worthless body is like a coat of armor; it suits you neither for winter nor for summer.

> Yet, this cumbersome companion is good for you because of the patience (that you must exercise in keeping it in check). Putting patience to work causes the heart to grow (in understanding).

The patience shown by the moon in the darkness of the night sky keeps it lit up; the patience shown by the rose as it sits near the thorn keeps it smelling nice.

Mathnawi VI, 1406–1408

When a person has expanded her vision, purified her heart, tamed her body, and learned the lessons that set her free from worry, sorrow, and stress, then she literally lives as if drunk with divine love. It doesn't mean that she becomes fruity or flighty in her demeanor like some poster child from the psychedelic '60s, but rather it means that in every endeavor, in every pastime and hobby, and in every part of her normal life, she sees the extraordinary within the ordinary. Work no longer becomes just a paycheck, but a means to give back to the world; family life takes on a new sweetness—the precious gifts of earthly love and companionship are finally recognized for the treasures that they are. Anger is mitigated; eventually it disappears altogether. Stress and uncertainty are defeated by the straight-arrow vision of the long view, and the desire to do injustice or indulge in hurtful things melts away under the radiant eye of unconditional love.

Footprints of the Master

Like most mystical poets of classical Islamic civilization, Rumi sometimes uses the imagery of drunkenness and wine as a metaphor for becoming dizzy in contemplating and fully realizing the depth of God's overwhelming love. It doesn't necessarily mean that each mystical poet drank wine, for very few did, as it was a forbidden act in the Islamic religion. It's a colorful analogy used to elicit the reader's attention.

In short, the goal of all religions, philosophies, and therapies finally becomes realized. The person transforms herself from within into a dynamic, thoughtful, caring, giving, balanced, and goal-oriented member of the human family. She sheds her own weaknesses and merges the self into the light from which all our souls sprang. We finally see the life preserver that's been thrown to us in the middle of a turbulent sea, and we no longer wish for any of the wreckage of our ship that may be floating around us. All we want to do is become servants of love. On this, Rumi wrote:

Serve (God) so you can become a lover. Serving (God) is a way to gain (God's love) for it (quickly) comes into play. The one who serves (God) wishes to be freed from (the impersonal nature) of destiny. The One who loves (God) never wishes for anything more (than that).

The worker is always looking to be wrapped in honor and to receive a salary; the lover is wrapped in the honor of seeing the Object of his love. Love isn't found in mere words or hearsay; Love is an ocean whose bottom you can't see. The drops of the sea can never be numbered; all the water in the seven seas is nothing compared with the Ocean (of God's Love).

Mathnawi V, 2728–2732

You're Worth the Effort

Rumi put forth the belief that human beings have a value deeper than their mere form or substance. He held that we all contain a gem, a gift from a single Source that we label the spirit, the subconscious, or the soul. Evidence abounds that there is more to the human mind than just the brainpower and emotions it applies to daily, mundane tasks. Rumi called upon people to latch on to those fleeting moments when deeper realization occurs, and then to embark on a quest to awaken that seed of expansive thought so it no longer shuts down under a crowd of worldly concerns. Let that inner consciousness become your identity, let it lead you forward in life so you can, by its wisdom, lead a life more satisfying than you could have ever had otherwise.

The task is not easy; it requires patience and determination, as well as a willingness to stand up whenever you're knocked down. And you don't have to go it alone; take a Master as your guide. Rumi put it thusly:

Unless you really want to keep stumbling on this path alone, then sharpen your sight on the dust of a spiritual master's foot.

Mathnawi IV, 3372

In other words, there is no virtue in unnecessary hardship on this journey of self-actualization; take a teacher—someone who specializes in spiritual knowledge—and learn from that teacher diligently. Along the way, you will learn to purify your heart and actions, and though it will require a lot of soul-searching and practice, the payoff is to gain the greatest treasure in the universe: reunion with the love that gave you a gem of a soul in the first place. Rumi advised this:

> The journey of the spirit wrecks the body's house, yet afterward it makes it whole again. It wrecks the house to dig out the treasure, and with that treasure, it builds a better house than before.

Mathnawi I, 306–307

The Least You Need to Know

◆ While Rumi was an orthodox Muslim throughout his life, he believed all people, no matter what their religion, have a soul from the same Source.

◆ Rumi believed human beings have both an angelic side and an animalistic side. The more people move toward their better nature, the closer to God they will be.

◆ Enlightenment can be sought without renouncing one's normal world. Enlightenment comes from living life more fully and with greater emphasis on the meaning of what one does.

◆ True peace comes when a person fully opens his or her soul from within to the Universal Love that is God.

Chapter 3

Rumi the Writer

In This Chapter

- ◆ Rumi's many literary works and how they complement each other
- ◆ The relationship between the *Divan* and the *Mathnawi*
- ◆ The teachings of the *Seven Sermons*
- ◆ The path of Rumi's evolution of thought seen through the lens of his writing endeavors

Rumi was a prolific author, poet, and preacher. In his nearly 70 years of life, he produced thousands of pages on a wide variety of topics and subject matters. Due to the popularity of his work, his books have survived remarkably intact to this day. He composed most of his work in the Persian language, which was the language of the educated and cultured. (He also wrote in Arabic, Greek, and Turkish.) In this chapter we will really begin to explore the depths of Rumi's written works. As you journey through subsequent chapters and they become increasingly dominated by Rumi's words (and less of mine), you will develop a working familiarity with the different sources from which these selections originate, while increasing your understanding and awareness of the path to enlightenment.

Rumi's kindness and expansive intellect are captured in this medieval Persian rendering of the venerable mystic.

The *Divan*

The first compilation of Rumi's work is the well-known book called the *Divan*. The word *divan* (or *diwan* in Arabic) was the literary term in classical Muslim civilization for an anthology of an author's works. There are many "divans" from antiquity produced by a whole host of authors. But whenever we use the term divan in this book, it refers only to Rumi's work.

Rumi began to compose elementary poetry in his mid- to late 20s, and he saved many of his compositions through the intervening years, thus giving us a record of the development of his thoughts. He didn't become "prolific" in the full sense of the word, however, until after his brief time spent with the enigmatic mystic, Shamsuddin of Tabriz. Rumi had formed such a strong bond with him in such a short time that when his friend disappeared, Rumi had no other outlet than to compose poetry to console the sudden emptiness he felt in his heart. These poems, along with some reworked earlier poetry and reflections, form the basis of Rumi's *Divan*. Yet it is also thought that Rumi kept adding to his *Divan* even into his most senior years.

🐾 Footprints of the Master

What made Shamsuddin of Tabriz so intense a person that he would have had such a profound effect on the otherwise sober-minded Rumi? As it turns out, Shamsuddin's father was a prominent leader of the militant Assassins, a heretical non-Muslim group that operated principally in Lebanon between the eighth and fourteenth centuries. (They were sort of like the ninjas of the Middle East—daggers for hire.) Shamsuddin's father who was coincidentally also named Jalaluddin, eventually renounced the teachings of this group and dedicated himself zealously to learning and promoting orthodox Islam. He sent his son, Shamsuddin, to study with orthodox theologians and ignited a desire within him to know the truth on as deep a level as possible. Shamsuddin earned the nickname "the flier" due to his constant wanderings. He was so charismatic that people responded to his preaching wherever he went.

One can see the development of Rumi's worldview and spiritual interests as they evolved in the *Divan*, which is something of a prequel to his last work, the *Mathnawi*. Even though at first glance Shamsuddin seems to take center stage in the *Divan*, his inclusion eventually transforms into something of a metaphor. After Rumi's initial burst of sorrow, as contained in his early odes of longing toward his long lost friend, he soon blossoms beyond that sense of personal loss and begins to address the collective human desire for God and for inner peace. Here is an example of one of the *Divan's* quatrains that expresses this idea.

> Clap your hands in joy for Him, by Whose hands foam alights upon the sea. Joy in Him leaves no room for affliction or misery. So listen to Him without your ears and speak to Him from within. Leave the tongue behind for its vulgar nature produces only pain.

From the *Divan*

🐾 Footprints of the Master

In honor of his friendship with the mysterious Shamsuddin, Rumi entitled his anthology, *Divan-i Shams-i Tabrizi*, with Shamsuddin's name prominently placed where Rumi's name, the real author of the work, should have been. Rumi's *Divan* is also known by the alternative title, *Divan-i Kabir*, or *The Grand Collection of Discourses*.

The *Divan*, as you will see, is truly a multifaceted work. It alternates between all the major human emotions of longing, fear, hope, joy, sadness, reunion, and ecstasy. While Rumi's *Mathnawi* (which we will discuss later) is recognized as a masterpiece of the spiritual realm, in the same way, his *Divan* is the song of the human heart magnified many times over.

Its Three Major Parts

The *Divan* is a collection of three types of writings: four-line quatrains, poems of half-line rhymes, and, finally, the longer odes that make up the bulk of the book. Here is a brief summary of each type:

◆ The Quatrains (*rubaiyat*) are brief four-line poems that speak on a whole host of topics in very concise and sometimes figurative language. They appear in a long train at the end of the *Divan*. There are about 2,000 of them presently, though only about 1,600 are thought to have been penned by Rumi. (The oldest manuscripts contain 400 fewer quatrains, so later followers presumably tacked on the rest.)

◆ The Extended Poems (*tarji'at*) are spiritual ruminations expressed in a rhymed structure generally of 13 syllables. There are 44 of these poems, which are made up of multiple sections strung loosely together on a common theme. They total about 1,700 verses.

◆ The Odes (*ghazals*) are ecstatic longings expressed in rhymed verses of various rhyme schemes. They are anywhere from 10 to 40 lines each. There are about 3,230 of these odes, totaling some 35,000 verses. These odes make up the overwhelming majority of the *Divan*'s contents.

The most common theme of the *Divan*, as noted before, involves the loss of that which makes one whole. For Rumi at that time, Shamsuddin was the missing key for his spiritual education. This led to Rumi's early concept of losing one's self in the endless depths of one's spiritual Master. Thus, this is an early principle of Rumi's evolving philosophy.

Later on, Rumi would realize that as much as another human being could be a "mirror of one's self," the truest form of tranquility came from seeking the Divine Presence, rather than union with a mere mortal. Thus, by the time of his writings in *Mathnawi*, the emphasis was on losing one's self in God. With that said, at the time of his grieving for Shamsuddin, Rumi used his literary abilities, as expressed in the *Divan*, to work through his deeply felt sense of loss.

Odes to Shamsuddin

Now let's take a look at some of Rumi's odes of longing that he wrote on behalf of Shamsuddin. In this first selection, Rumi writes of the effect that finding Shamsuddin had upon his life and very essence. In metaphorical language it takes us from Rumi's first chance meeting with Shamsuddin through their first inseparable weeks together.

> In the early morning, a moon arose in the sky. Then it came down from on high and looked at me. Just as the falcon snatches up a bird during the hunt, that moon snatched me up and traversed through the heavens.
>
> When I looked at myself, I saw no one there, for in that moon my body had become ethereal spirit, like a soul is born. When I traveled on with this soul of mine, I saw nothing save the moon, until all the secret mysteries of faith were revealed.
>
> The nine spheres in the heavens all came together in that moon; my own body became completely submerged in the sea. The sea was filled with waves that crashed all around. Wisdom then arose and shouted out loud; that's what happened to me.
>
> Foam arose on the sea, and with every fleck of foam, a form appeared and a shape emerged. Every fleck of foam was a body; whoever among them received a sign from that sea melted instantly back within it and turned to spirit in that ocean. Without the remarkable power of Shams, the truthful one from Tabriz, no one could have ever seen this moon or become one with the sea.

Here, Rumi records what spending time with Shamsuddin meant for him in his daily life. The pair used to sit together in Rumi's garden and talk for hours. Their ideas were a perfect fit together; where one would begin a thought, the other would complete it. They had that rare and precious gift—a perfect friendship.

> The most joyful times were when we sat together, just you and I, on the veranda; two forms, two faces, yet one soul, you and I.
>
> The fruits of the orchard and the singing of the birds offered us the Water of Life as soon as we entered the garden, you and I. The stars of the night sky came to watch us, and we, ourselves, revealed the moon to them, you and I.
>
> There was you, and then there was I, without there being any sense of just a "you" or an "I," due to our delightful unity. Completely unconcerned with foolish stories and distractions that may have floated by, we were locked in our happiness, just you and I.
>
> All the birds of the sky pecked at sweet sugar in a place from where we laughed, you and I. Even more amazing than that—you and I were in one corner of the world over here, while in the same instant, we were both in Iraq or Khorosan, you and I.
>
> One form we shared here on earth, and another form we will share over there, in everlasting Paradise—the Realm of all that is sweet—the home of you, and the home of I.

Rumi's References

The name *Shamsuddin* means "The Rising Sun of the Faith." Ironically, Rumi often refers to Shamsuddin as "the moon" in the *Divan*.

In this next ode, Rumi writes of the time when Shamsuddin was planning to run away from Konya due to the insults and taunts he received from Rumi's jealous students:

> I've heard that you're planning to leave. Don't do it. I've heard that you intend to grace a new friend with your love. Don't do it.

While in the world, you're a strange one, and at the same time, you've never known what it's like to be a stranger.

What are you planning to do, you heartless fool? Don't do it. Don't steal yourself away from me, don't go to strangers.

You're looking secretly at others. Don't do it. O moon for whom the heavens are bewildered, you're making me distraught and bewildered, too! Don't do it.

Where is the promise and where is the agreement you made with me? You're abandoning your word and your pledge. Don't do it.

Why are you making promises and offering defenses? Why are you using your vows like a shield and a weapon? Don't do it.

Finally, Rumi penned this ode on behalf of his lament and sorrow after Shamsuddin disappeared. The sun mentioned here is the translation of Shamsuddin's name, and as you can see, Rumi is heartbroken at his separation from his closest confidant.

Last night I asked a star if it had any news of you. "Show me," I said, "all the ways I gave service to that moonbeam." Then I bowed my head low and said, "Now take all of this, my service, and present it to the sun, which makes hard stone shine like gold from its heat."

Then I bared my chest to that star and showed it all my wounds. "Tell him about me," I cried, "for he's the beloved who feasts on blood." Then I rocked myself back and forth to still the frightened child within my heart. Doesn't a child go to sleep when his cradle is gently swayed?

Give my heart sweet mother's milk; save me from its weeping, O You who help a hundred helpless souls like mine every day. The first and last home of every heart is in Your city of unison. How long will You keep this listless heart in exile? I won't say another word, save to relieve the ache in my mind. O Cup-bearer, make drunk my forlorn eyes.

An image of Shamsuddin of Tabriz on the cover of an illustrated Persian copy of the Divan, c. 1503.

A Selection of Quatrains

Some of Rumi's shorter quatrains from the *Divan*, as follows, speak of loss, while others speak of hope, reflecting the many facets of Rumi's talent.

When I Became Free

I spent years copying others in my quest to know myself. Within my heart, I never knew what to do. When I could see no longer, I heard my name being called from somewhere. Then I took a walk outside.

Leave Me

My heart, leave me if you cannot stand the pain.

Leave me, for the streets are full of homeless lovers. My soul, if you're not afraid, then come to me, but if you're scared, then leave me be, for your work is not here.

You Are My All

If my head knows one thing for certain, it's you. As poor as I am, you're all that I hold dear. No matter how I see myself, I'm nothing at all. Whatever I may be is entirely due to you.

Speak Not with Fools

Leave the ignorant to themselves. Hold on to the robes of the sensible. Never waste your breath on an ignorant fool. Even a mirror will rust when dropped in water.

Time Brings All High Ones Low

Time cuts short all sounds and quarrels. The wolf of death cuts to pieces all who flock together. Everyone has some kind of pride within themselves, yet, the blow of death strikes everyone down.

A Prelude to the *Mathnawi*

You may get the impression that the *Divan* is only about Rumi's sense of loss, but it also contains many fine passages that probe into the science of spirituality, if you will. The following selection reveals how the *Divan* was, in reality, something of a practice-run for the monumental *Mathnawi* that was to come later on. By this I mean that Rumi's emphasis on spirituality for its own sake, as expressed in the *Mathnawi*, gets its first articulation in these early poems, which show the future potential of the Master to write on love and the spirit from an even higher perspective.

> Enter here with us; we're the lovers of God. Let us open the gate to the Garden of Love for you. Become a member of our home, like a shadow, so we can be neighbors of the Sun.
>
> Even though we're invisible, like the soul in the world, and even though we're discreet like the love of lovers—yet still our nature is always evident to you, since we're both hidden and clear, just like the soul.
>
> Whatever you happen to say of us, such as, "You're this or that"— look even higher, since we're even higher than that!

You're like a stream, but a whirlpool has imprisoned you under the ground. Enter here with us, for we're like a torrent rushing onward to the Sea.

Ever since we've gambled everything away by losing ourselves completely, we know nothing more than books that teach us how to know nothing at all!

The *Seven Sermons*

Throughout his life, Rumi gave many sermons in the mosques of Konya and many addresses and speeches to gatherings of his students, followers, and others. On seven of these more auspicious occasions, either Rumi's son, Sultan Walad, or his top student, Husamuddin Chelebi, recorded what the Master said. These seven recorded sermons, together, are known as the *Majalis-i Saba'*, which translates as the *Seven Sermons*.

Each of these seven speeches centers upon an important saying, or *hadith*, of the Prophet Muhammad and is expounded upon with a wide variety of anecdotes, examples, and persuasive arguments. In tone, these speeches are more businesslike and less like the poetry that characterizes Rumi's other works.

Here is a brief summary of the contents of each of the *Seven Sermons* of Rumi. They appear as well-organized speeches in all respects.

- ◆ **Sermon 1:** Believers should follow the example and way of Prophet Muhammad. Untold rewards will accrue to the benefit of those who adhere to the Prophet's way in uncertain times.

- ◆ **Sermon 2:** Whoever preserves himself from falling into sinful ways and who avoids arrogance, one of the worst sins, will gain spiritual richness from God. Real wealth is a contented heart. Followers of the Truth avoid greed, arrogance, and revenge, and they advance their knowledge through education.

- ◆ **Sermon 3:** Pure and sincere faith will propel a person toward honest worship of God. Prayers should be performed in a humble frame of mind, and God's help should be sought in all affairs.

- **Sermon 4:** God loves those who are pure at heart. God favors those who are humble and who love Him rather than the material world. God loves those who repent to Him if they ever commit a sin. God accepts the repentance of the sincere and erases their sins.

- **Sermon 5:** The only way a person can be saved from the pitfalls of the world is through religious knowledge. Those who know nothing of religion are like an empty scarecrow. Those who acquire religious knowledge are like doctors who heal others. Knowledge is the weapon a believer uses against sin.

- **Sermon 6:** The world is like a trap that captures any who cling too closely to it. Those who focus themselves only upon the world of the present pass through life unaware of the bigger picture. They are heedless and do not perform the tasks that God would have them do. They can only expect destruction in the next life.

- **Sermon 7:** The only way a person can understand her soul and how her motivations work is through knowledge and reason. When a person uses her mind to delve deeply within herself, she can finally begin the journey toward becoming beloved of God.

The following is an excerpt from the first of these speeches:

> The prosperity and wealth of a fine mansion is a chain upon the restless soul. Indeed, the soul is deceived by such golden chains, and thus, it can't pass over the desert (of this world and into Heaven). It remains stuck in its oasis. Even though its oasis may seem like a paradise, in fact it's a hell. Although it may seem like a rose in appearance, yet in fact it's a poisonous snake. All you who are innocent! Beware of that rose-colored life, for that kind of rose is in hellfire. Indeed, it's a hell in and of itself, and this becomes evident when a full discussion reveals it for what it truly is.

> From the *Seven Sermons*

The Letters of Rumi

Islamic civilization was a society that placed a high value on preserving written records. In Rumi's time, it had already been a well-established practice to collect the letters of scholars together and publish them in book form. Thus, Rumi's students saved many of his letters and collated about 150 of them in a book. This collection of letters is called the *Maktubat*, or *Writings*.

In keeping with Rumi's religious and philosophical nature, all of these letters are liberally sprinkled with references from the Qur'an, the sayings of Muhammad, anecdotes, quotes from famous writers, and poems. Rumi's letters, which were written to rulers, friends, students, and others, fall into three basic categories that can be summarized as follows:

◆ **Letters of Advice.** These were most often addressed to government officials to exhort them to remain righteous and to do good deeds in the conduct of their duties. Sometimes he wrote letters of this sort to friends and relatives.

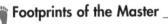

Footprints of the Master

The three most influential Persian poets of all time, Fariduddin 'Attar, Hakim Sana'i, and Jalaluddin Rumi, were all Sunni Muslims, while Persia (Iran) today is over 90 percent Shi'a Muslim.

◆ **Letters of Recommendation.** Like any well-respected professor, Rumi wrote letters of recommendation to help people get jobs or receive grants from the government.

◆ **Letters of Religious Rulings.** Rumi received many requests for religious guidance and rulings on a wide variety of topics.

Let's look at an example of an occasion that prompted Rumi to write a letter. Rumi had gotten his son, Sultan Walad, married off to Fatimah, the daughter of his good friend, Salahuddin Zarqubi. The newlyweds later had a fight, and there was a period of estrangement between them. Rumi wrote a letter to Fatimah in which he told her that he supported her side in the disagreement and that she was fully justified in her position. He then told her that he felt sorry for her sadness, and that he always had the utmost respect for her father, who had recently passed away. Rumi wrote that he was so indebted to her father that, "Only the treasury of God Most High could repay him for the gratitude I feel."

Rumi then went on to say that he didn't want her to hide any of her suffering, and that it would help him to convince his son to be reasonable and reconcile with her. He backed up his concern by saying that if his son didn't relent of his anger, then he would give up his love for his own son, refrain from returning his greetings, and he wouldn't allow his son to attend his funeral. He then wrote, "I wish that you never would have been made to suffer or feel sad. God, may He be glorified, will help you, and the servants of God will help you, too." (The pair eventually reconciled.) Rumi included this poem in his letter:

> May the splendors of Salahuddin rise again, and be poured into the eyes of the lovers. May every soul that's been purified and become even purer than that, be mingled with the dust of Salahuddin.

Whatever Is in *This* Is in *That*

Various discussions, teaching sessions, and ordinary lectures of Rumi's were recorded and gathered together in a book entitled, *Fihi Ma Fihi*, an Arabic phrase that means, *"What's in This Is in That."* Many scholars believe that it's something of a play on words, a funny way of saying, "Whatever you read in *this* book is in *that* book" (referring to the *Mathnawi*).

The recordings are not official sermons, like in the *Seven Sermons*, but they are a goldmine of Rumi's thoughts and advice nonetheless. In all, there are 70 separate essays of varying length. The following are some excerpts taken from this collection.

How Destiny Steers Our Way

> There once was a man leading the prayers, and while doing so he happened to recite the line from the Qur'an that said, "The Bedouins are stubborn in their disbelief and hypocrisy." As it happened, a Bedouin chief was present. (He became angry) and slapped the prayer leader on the side of his head. Then, in the second half of the prayer, the prayer leader recited the next line that

said, "Yet among the Bedouins are some who believe in God and the Last Day." The Bedouin chief exclaimed proudly, "So there! That slap has taught you better manners!" We're always getting slaps from the unseen world. Whatever we may plan to do, we're kept away from it by a slap, and we do something else.

Excerpted from *Discourse 49*

The Eternal Quest for Love

Wherever you are and in whatever condition you may be, work hard to always be a lover (of God), and a passionate one at that. Once you've taken ownership of love, you'll always be a lover, even if you be in the grave, at the resurrection or in Paradise forever. When you've planted wheat, wheat will surely grow. Wheat will be in the storeroom and wheat will be baked in the oven. Majnun wanted to write a letter to Layla. He picked up a pen and wrote these lines:

Your name is on my tongue,

Your image is in my sight,

Thoughts of you linger in my heart:

So to whom shall I write?

Your image dwells within my sight, your name never leaves my tongue, your remembrance dwells deep with my soul, so to whom shall I write a letter, given that you already occupy all those places. The pen broke and the page was torn in half.

Rumi's References

The story of Layla and Majnun is a spiritual *Romeo and Juliet* for Muslims. It was composed in the seventh or eighth century, and it tells the tale of a young man named Qays who falls in love with a girl named Layla. Her father refuses to allow Qays to marry his daughter and thus the stricken lover gradually descends into a kind of madness, even as Layla does, too. Sufis have generally likened the quest of Qays (now called *Majnun*, or *Crazy One*) as a metaphor for the imperfect human search for God.

There are many people who have hearts filled with words like this, yet they cannot express them aloud, even though they're lovers in constant search for this. That's not to be unexpected, and it in no way is an impediment to love. As a matter of fact, the most important matter is the heart and an unceasing passion for love. Even as a baby is in love with milk, gaining nourishment and strength thereby, still the baby cannot describe or explain what milk is, or offer this simple utterance, saying, "I feel great from drinking milk, and I feel miserable and malnourished when I'm away from it." In spite of all this, the baby wants that milk with its very heart and soul. On the other hand, a grown adult, who can describe milk and all its qualities a thousand ways, gains no similar pleasure when he drinks it.

Excerpted from *Discourse 44*

Whose Fault Is It if You're Bored?

If I say nothing, then people who come to me will get bored. However, when I talk to them, I have to talk on their level, so I get bored. Then they go and say all kinds of bad things about me, that I got bored of them and ran away. How can the firewood run away from the cooking pot? The pot may flee when it can't stand the heat of the fire, but when the fire runs away, it's not because it's really running away; rather, it's turning itself down because it knows the pot is weak. Therefore, despite all appearances, it's always the pot that runs away. So when I run away it's really them running away. I'm like a mirror, and if they want to leave, it's reflected back in me. I'm running away for them! A mirror only shows others their reflection. If they think I'm bored, the boredom is really theirs! Boredom is a sign of weakness, and this is no place for boredom or fatigue.

Excerpted from *Discourse 21*

As you can see in this collection of Rumi's talks, there is a generous amount of analogy, stories, poems, historical or literary allusion, and advice. In a way, reading his speeches, as they're collected in *Fihi Ma Fihi*, is a way to be able to sit in on the lectures of the Master. Whereas the *Divan* is an emotional and ecstatic experience, *Fihi Ma Fihi* is more of an intellectual, spiritual, and thoughtful one.

The *Mathnawi*

The *Mathnawi*, or *Rhymed Couplets*, is Rumi's last and most famous work. It consists of six lengthy books of poetry (each containing several thousand lines of text), set up in a teaching-style format designed to convey some important lesson. It's the only one of Rumi's works that he deliberately composed in chronological order for a single purpose. By way of comparison, the *Divan* is a collection of many different types of poems and odes organized loosely with a certain kind of randomness to it, whereas the *Mathnawi* is a unified series with a central purpose.

Rumi began this monumental project at the urging of his top student, Husamuddin Chelebi, who is purported to have asked his Master to leave behind a book that his students could learn from, similar to the monumental works of Hakim Sanai and Fariduddin 'Attar. Rumi, it is said, instantly pulled a paper from out of his turban that had the first 18 lines of a poem written on it. This was the first poem and official opening of the entire *Mathnawi* collection. This selection is known today as "The Lament of the Reed (Flute)." Here is its translation:

> Listen to the reed and the story that it tells, for it speaks of separation: "Ever since I've been taken from the reed-bed," it sighs, "men and women have joined with me in mourning my loss."

> "Bring me a broken heart, torn from separation, so that I can explain to it what suffering from unfulfilled desire truly is. Anyone who's ever gone far from where he belongs seeks to return to the place where he used to be."

> "And so, I cry in every gathering, while I cavort with all in both good times and bad. However, all who become my friend do so for their own selfish reasons. They never seek to know my secret from within. My secret isn't far from my sorrow, but eyes and ears have not the vision to see it."

> The body cannot hide from the soul, nor can the soul hide from the body, yet the soul isn't allowed to be seen. The reed's lament is like a fire—it's certainly not from the wind (of the player)! Whoever doesn't have this fire inside, let him be as nothing!

It's the fire of Love that's in the reed, and it's the ferment of Love that's in the wine. The reed is the company of all who've been separated from a friend; its melodies tear our veils (of sadness) away.

Who has ever seen such a poison and a cure like the reed? Who has ever seen a friend as sympathetic or as desirous as the reed? The reed recites tales of a hot-blooded path; it recites tales of Majnun's passion. Only those beyond their senses get this feeling; the tongue has no customer save for the ear.

In our sorrow, the days (of our lives) become like nights; our days travel along with our distress. If our days come to an end, then let them go! For it doesn't matter in the least! But you—you can remain, for none are as pure as you.

Anyone can be satisfied with water—except for a fish, and anyone who lacks his daily bread feels the length of his days. No one who is green understands what it means to be ripened. Therefore, my words must be brief. Good-bye!

Mathnawi I, 1–18

The Secret Is Out!

The *Mathnawi* is set up in the classic style of a Sufi teaching manual. It conveys its message almost entirely through stories of varying length. Like many such collections that came before it, the *Mathnawi* contains within its tales references to the Qur'an, the sayings of Muhammad, Muslim history, famous saints and sinners, poetic allusions, and tales of animals and fantastic events. What most readers and fans of Rumi don't realize—*shhhh*, I'm going to tell you a secret—is that most of the poems you read in those "Rumi books" you see everywhere were actually not written as briefly as they're presented. In other words, you may read an isolated poem of a few lines from the *Mathnawi* and feel that Rumi wrote the poem just like that—as a stand-alone poem. This isn't usually the case. Nearly all the Rumi poems you read in the popular books were literally lifted out of larger passages and stories. (To be fair, I also have followed this technique to enable the reader to see snapshots of Rumi's wisdom.)

Here is an example of what I mean. Any presenter of Rumi poems can present the following text by itself, and it would be sufficient by itself for many hours of deep reflection.

> A crooked hair veiled the sky.
>
> So how would it be if all your parts were crooked?
>
> Straighten yourself with the help of the righteous, O you who would follow the straight path.
>
> Don't turn aside from any door in which the righteous dwell.
>
> *Mathnawi* II, 119–121

This text, however, is really part of a larger teaching story that is 11 verses long. It begins with a man incorrectly claiming to have seen the new crescent moon that starts the fasting month of Ramadan. But then the caliph proves the man was wrong, because a stray hair had been draped over his eyes. The lesson, then, is not to boast of what comes from one's own senses, but to seek a second opinion and be humble. Thus, whenever you're reading any Rumi poem, particularly if it comes from the *Mathnawi*, keep in mind that it may have a larger background story surrounding it. If you feel the thirst to know more, then you can acquire a full translation of the *Mathnawi*. That's what I did when I fell in love with Rumi's work so many years ago.

Wisdom of the Ages _____

A Persian writer of the later classical period named Jami' once wrote of Rumi: "Let the fires of hell be forbidden for the one who reads the *Mathnawi* day and night. What can I say about this great man? He wasn't a prophet, yet he had a scripture."

Beyond a Mere Mortal

If you will remember, when Rumi was mourning the loss of his spiritual friend Shamsuddin, he composed much of the *Divan* to assuage his feelings of despair. This was when he thought a person only needed to lose him or herself in a spiritual Master to achieve peace. Many years later, when Rumi grew beyond this doctrine, realizing that the soul could only be content when it opened itself to the truth of God, he began work on the *Mathnawi*. When the work was just beginning, perhaps out of habit, his secretary Husamuddin asked his Master if he would also speak of Shamsuddin in this new book as he did in his prior work. Rumi composed these lines in answer:

> It's better that an old friend remains hidden.
>
> Come, listen to what these stories contain.
>
> It's far better for the secrets of lovers to be told, in other stories and in tales of old.
>
> *Mathnawi* I, 135–136

In other words, there would be no talk of Shamsuddin, or any other person who made a similarly profound impact on Rumi's life. The *Mathnawi* was to be the pure exposition of a lifetime of knowledge that points to communion with one's inner self and a realization of the expansive nature of the Source of all being. As Rumi put it: "O seeker of the Sea of the Spirit, come to the *Mathnawi*. Come to the *Mathnawi*, so you can always see, that there's an ocean of spirit within it."

The Reach of the *Mathnawi*

The *Mathnawi* has influenced the cultures of every Muslim land from Turkey to India and on into central Asia and beyond. Such is its influence that when the famous Turkish poet, Yahya Kemal (d. 1958), was asked how it was possible that the Ottoman Turks made it all the way to the gates of Vienna in their drive deep into Europe, he replied, "It's because we ate rice and read the *Mathnawi*."

On the other side of the Middle East, one of the most influential figures in Pakistani history, Allamah Muhammad Iqbal (d. 1938), repeatedly referred to Rumi as his "spiritual leader" in his own poems. When Kemal Ataturk (d. 1938) tried to secularize Turkey by force in the early twentieth century, the first sign that he was willing to relent in his war on religion came when he visited Konya and the tomb of Rumi. He described the feeling he got from being close to Rumi's mosque and tomb as a time of inner excitement. Rumi's works also went a long way toward converting the untamed Mongols to Islam a century after their first invasions of the civilized world in the thirteenth century.

Today, Rumi's works have been translated into dozens of languages, and recordings of spoken Rumi poems have even made it onto Billboard's Top 20 list. It has been said that Rumi is the best-selling poet in the English-speaking world at this time, thanks in large part to the efforts of such Rumi translators as Reynold Nicholson, A. J. Arberry, Coleman Barks, Kabir, and Camille Helminski.

So what did Rumi think the impact of the *Mathnawi* would be? He wrote, "After us, the *Mathnawi* will be a Shaykh (respected leader), and it will point the way toward the true path for those who search for it, and those who rule and those who lead others." Strangely enough, more people find solace in his words and insights now than he ever could have imagined.

The Least You Need to Know

◆ Rumi's poetry, odes, letters, sermons, and speeches are recorded in many books.

◆ Rumi's *Divan* evolves from expressions of longing and personal loss into the human desire for God and inner peace.

◆ The speeches of Rumi contained in the *Seven Sermons* are drawn from sayings of the Prophet Muhammad.

◆ The *Mathnawi* is Rumi's most voluminous as well as most structured work, designed specifically to teach important lessons.

Part 2

Nothing for Something Is Everything

Popular songs and writers often speak of the need for people to liberate themselves from the worries and cares of the world. The dream within us all often begins with the desire to break away, to strike out on our own path, and to get some meaning in our quest for something real. As fate would have it, Rumi is our perfect guide!

People often fail to recognize what's holding them back and don't recognize the spark of life that's just inside, waiting to burst forth in full splendor. Inner demons of fear and uncertainty can tie people to the ever-changing fortunes of this world. In this part, through a masterful use of anecdotes, similes, and metaphors, Rumi teaches you how to truly free yourself and begin your search with a lightened yet purposeful mind.

Chapter 4

The Forgotten Self

In This Chapter

- ◆ Discovering how Rumi exposes the existence of the soul
- ◆ Uncovering the "real you" and why it's so important
- ◆ Exploring the concept and perception of time
- ◆ Accepting yourself for the treasure that you are, without regrets

The beginning of any search, regardless of the object of the quest, is to identify exactly what is being sought after. Who goes out of his house and says, "I'm looking for 'X' (you fill in the blank)," with no idea of how "X" is going to contribute to his life? Who goes to work for reasons other than satisfaction and/or a paycheck? While it is true that a journey of a thousand miles begins with one step, the assumption is that the traveler has some idea of where she would like to end up. The same holds true for any spiritually oriented endeavor. A person may seek solace in prayer, yet he can only achieve it if he utters his prayers with the conviction that they may be answered. Likewise, when a person wants to heal a wound within his soul, he must know that such a process brings the promise of a resolution.

In the same way, mystics of every religion point out that the journey of self-discovery must begin with an inward trek. A person can go all the way to India and sit at the feet of a wise sage, only to find out that she's no better off than if she stayed home and watched TV. She can perform a pilgrimage to some holy place and return feeling completely unchanged for her trouble. It's not going somewhere that brings healing to our inner self; rather, it's when we climb the mountain peak that is at the root of our psyche and enter in to the obscure grotto of our true essence. Only then can we begin to make progress in our search for meaning, contentment, and spiritual solace. So the attainment of happiness and fullness of spirit requires no physical journey of thousands of miles, for the path to self-awareness begins in the least obvious place of all—in the very space our body occupies, even if that space is right there in our very own living room!

Rumi especially would agree, for he spent the last half of his life in the same town, living in the same house, and traveling nowhere—and that was during the most spiritually rewarding part of his life. The journey toward inner peace, then, begins with the most overlooked treasure of all—it begins with you. In this chapter we will explore how the "real you" is easily hidden yet ever-present, and how Rumi expresses this presence and yearning for our inner self.

The Overlooked Treasure

Have you ever felt that you didn't know who you were? Not the mundane things like your name, your history, your job, or your daily routines, but knowing who the real "you" is, deep down, in that spot inside, which nobody knows about but you. Has there ever been a time when you literally "woke up" from your busy life, even just for a moment, and suddenly felt like a swimmer coming up for air after having been under for far too long? Have you ever found yourself becoming unusually afraid that you might be missing out on living your "real" life, and knowing who you really are? Did a casual glance at something awaken unusual thoughts somewhere from deep within you that left you yearning for more depth? What you may have experienced in those instances was the inner spark of your true self, fighting to get out from under the heap of worldly demands that may have been unwittingly piled upon it.

What would cause an inner feeling of yearning to erupt from within us out of nowhere like that? Could it be that despite all we may have achieved or done or learned, we've somehow neglected something that's simply unwilling to remain on the sidelines forever? Perhaps we have overlooked the real treasure of this life in favor of material shapes that pass in and out of our hands.

This world is filled with religions, philosophies, ideologies, and psychological teachings that all speak of an inner identity, an inner consciousness, and the importance of getting in touch with who we are in the inner recesses of our minds. Could it be that we've achieved so much materially in this world that we've forgotten to, or how to, get in touch with our own innate spirituality?

Let's look at the sum total of our lives and see what could make us feel in need of a private liberation at this point. We spent our first years as a child in the constant haze of a dream-like existence, ever dependent on those who look after us. As we entered the adolescent years, a growing awareness of our lack of "freedom" gnawed at the edges of our psyche, sometimes leading us to rebel or challenge the powers that held sway over our lives. Angst, dreams, hormones, and adrenaline were on high, and there seemed to be no relief in sight on a constantly out-of-reach horizon. Then we had those few exciting years between high school and adult life, in which we felt as if we were really, truly alive. We made mistakes, learned lessons, and made more mistakes. As time passed on, some of us fell into a rut and others seemed to take off, and then the pattern sometimes reversed itself. Later, as we grow more mature (or immature), we settle in to our increasingly rigid opinions, habits, and values. By the time we get around to starting our "grown-up" lives, we've scarcely had time to catch our breath and ask, "What the heck just happened?" Rumi wrote of this very same phenomenon in these words:

> Is it any wonder that the spirit doesn't remember its own (ancient) home, in which it lived and emerged from so long before?

> This sleep-inducing world is wrapped around (the spirit) just as the clouds blot out the stars. (The soul) has traveled through so many cities, and the dust still hasn't been cleared from its senses.

Likewise, it hasn't made any serious effort to purify itself and take a good look at the past, so that its heart can cast a glance through the opening of mystery, allowing it to see the beginning and the end with an open eye.

Mathnawi IV, 3632–3636

Indeed, life has a way of throwing us for a loop beyond the drowsiness it induces in our souls. No sooner do we settle in to our routines than we suddenly find that the pace of time seems to speed up! With this enters the dreaded feeling of running out of time, and our inner self begins to panic. Some call it a mid-life crisis, while others call it wanderlust; others even bring out such terms as mental breakdown, life-stress, or anxiety. Perhaps it's our soul telling us to look to it for refuge after being neglected for so long! We take and take out of our inner reservoir, as we struggle along in this life, but how do we replenish our authentic self and feed our soul? Rumi says this:

Not a moment passes without your soul struggling with its own death, so in that struggle look to your faith!

Your life is like a purse filled with gold; every day and night sees the money-changer counting out the coins.

(God) counts (the coins) and gives gold to us freely, until the purse is emptied and the eclipse of death appears.

If you keep taking away from a mountain, without putting anything back, then the mountain will one day disappear from that kind of one-sided transfer.

So then put an equal amount of breath back for every one you take, so you can obey the verse (of the Qur'an that says,) " … *fall down in worship and draw yourself near*," for in that way you will gain what you seek.

Mathnawi III, 123–127

Scattered Time

Time and its passing is a relentless reminder to our soul of its ultimate passing, and it impels the soul ever harder to break free. Consider the bittersweet reality that a year as a 14-year-old lasts forever, but the same year for an adult goes by in what seems a matter of months! Why is this so? Well, if it's true that time flies when you're having fun, then adult life must be inordinately joyous! But is it? Is every day filled with bubbling laughter and meaningful experiences? Perhaps there are days like that, but what of the other kinds of days—the days of worry, hardship, drudgery, stress, anxiety, and just plain work? You'd think they would put a drag on our sense of the passage of time, yet the days whiz by nonetheless.

Therefore, it's not that we're so happy everyday that makes life such a blur; rather, it's something else entirely—and it's robbing us of our chance to feel truly alive. That something is our undue focus on everything and everyone except our own inner selves. In running to pick up the pieces of other people's lives, we often leave our own puzzle unsolved!

Wisdom of the Ages

Another Eastern mystical poet named Hafiz (d. 1390) wrote of the importance of unshackling one's desire for truth in these words: "Why abstain from love, when like a beautiful goose leaving for the winter, someday your soul, too, will leave this summer camp? Why abstain from happiness, when like a lion on the prowl, your heart is getting closer, and will one day see that the divine prey was always even nearer?"

There's a story of an old Duchess, who had every benefit in the world both materially and socially, and who upon her deathbed said, "I would give everything I own, for just a little more time." A contented soul would not have spoken such words, thereby demonstrating how the material world scatters our focus and leaves us unsatisfied. How many people have reached the pinnacle of their power and failed to remember that their life does not last forever? When the end is near, suddenly all the lost time and wasted pursuits come back to remembrance.

A life lived without focus is also a life lived without love. Love is not so cheap as to be merely the attraction of one fleshly body to another. Real love is deeper than that. Love binds the soul to its reality, to its transcendence. Without that inner love and joy in the soul, all we do is merely busy ourselves with tasks—one diversion after another—until we're stopped in our tracks by our ultimate doom. Rumi put this best when he wrote the following:

> Your thoughts are spread out over a hundred important affairs, over thousands of desires and innumerable matters great and small.
>
> You have to unite all these (scattered) parts through the agency of love, so that in the end you can become as sweet as (the fabled cities) of Samarqand and Damascus.
>
> When you've become one (in your focus), step by step coming out of your confusion, then and only then will it be possible to have the King set His seal upon you.
>
> *Mathnawi* IV, 3288–3290

Time Is the Reminder

The old adage tells us, "Here today, gone tomorrow." Indeed, truer words were never spoken! If you think about it, what do you really own in this world? More so, what possessions do you hold in your hands that compare in value with your inner peace and well-being? If mere things don't make you eternally happy, why spend years getting a good job just so you can purchase expensive baubles like gold or diamonds? We should quit our jobs and hunt for plain rocks to satisfy our need to hold material things in our hands. We can then carry them in our hands all day long, being as cheap and plentiful as they are! Ah, but we're picky in what we choose to hold, however, what we hold, whether a gold ring or a broken seashell, will slip from our grasp sooner or later. How can anything here in this world make us truly happy? In the end, as Rumi quoted the Prophet Muhammad saying, "True wealth doesn't come from an abundance of things, but from a contented mind."

The authentic self desires to come out, see the light of day, and lift itself out of the chasms of material deception, temporary distraction, and inevitable disappointment within which our shallow desires have buried it. The authentic self says, "Come as you are." Whereas the shallow self says, "What did you bring me? Are you sure it's good enough?" Embarking upon the process that ultimately leads to the release of your inner spirit shouldn't be delayed a moment longer, once you know its importance and once you finally realize that you may have been neglecting it. There isn't much time allotted to us in this world as it is. If you saw a pile of gold just waiting to be given to you, would you say you're too accustomed to holding your old rags to accept it? Would you say you're too busy to take the gold right now? Rather, you would drop whatever you're holding in an instant for what you would recognize as far, far more valuable. Look upon your inner peace and well-being likewise. Is it dearer to you than the worry, anxiety, and boredom you may already hold? We often say, "Life is too short to waste." Shouldn't we then take that message to heart and focus on the real treasure of existence, rather than exclusively on mere material success and goods? Rumi writes the following:

> Just look at yourself, how you're so afraid of becoming nothing.
>
> Know that nothingness is also afraid (that you might become something).
>
> If you're reaching out for worldly honor and success, it's merely from the latent fears (of death) you suffer from within your agonized spirit.
>
> Other than love for God, the Most Beautiful, all things are laced in the agony of the spirit, even if they seem as sweet as sugar.
>
> What is the agony of the spirit? To move toward death and never to have taken a hold of the Water of Life.
>
> *Mathnawi* I, 3684–3687

Your inner spirit is where your true wealth lies. Impediments to knowing and unleashing it are all those things you sacrifice your happiness for. But what is the cost of embarking on the road to tranquility of mind, heart, and soul? Do you need to leave your life, your family, or your interests behind to achieve harmony within yourself? Of course not; they aren't what's standing

Rumi's References

Rumi often speaks of the spirit and its essential nourishing qualities with the metaphor of water. In the parched Middle East, this allegory of the "Water of Life" would have been a very powerful visual image in the minds of Rumi's listeners.

in your way, even if you think they are. The impediment is always in a deeper place—a place no one can see but you, because it's inside of you. Indeed, the focus of the mind can get lost in materialism, circumstances, and responsibilities and is forgetful of its ultimate destiny. And while it seems an easy statement to make, that we need to look within to regain our inner sense of balance, however, it's much, much harder to actually peer into one's own inner psyche. This is what Rumi wrote:

> A thorn in the foot is hard enough to find, so how much harder would it be to find a thorn in the heart? Answer me that!
>
> If every unlucky person could find the thorn in his heart, then how could sadness ever prevail over him?
>
> *Mathnawi* I, 152–153

There Is Death in a Life Without Life

A nameless one begins each day as usual: up at 6:30 A.M., out of the house by 7:15 A.M., and on the job by 8 A.M. The rest of the day progresses equally as routine: work, have lunch, more work, drive home, in the door by 6:15 P.M., do home stuff, watch TV, go to bed. The next day, it starts all over. This goes on five, sometimes six days a week, 50 weeks a year (minus a couple of weeks vacation days likely scattered here and there). This goes on for 20 to 30 years with maybe a few career changes along the way. Then retirement, shuffleboard, and bingo—you know the story from there.

This kind of lifecycle describes what most of us experience, albeit with different variables and details: moments of fleeting success and satisfaction, punctuated by times of trial and tribulation. This is the carousel of life—a cycle repeated generation after generation. Some people seem to find genuine happiness in it, while most just survive. Sounds pretty bleak, doesn't it? But this realization opens a whole host of questions about life and its meaning (or lack thereof). What is a human being entitled to in his or her life? Is there any way to make a mundane life more fulfilling? If we have such a wonderful brain, how do we make it work for us and find some relief? What's the secret that we so often hear about—the secret to this so-called happy life?

Wisdom of the Ages

People can get locked in their familiar routines. When something unusual happens, however, it can suddenly awaken new feelings within us. And if we don't catch them in time, they may slip away as we settle back into our normal pace of life. For Rumi, that moment of opportunity came when a frantic dervish named Shamsuddin stopped him by chance in the market and asked him a seemingly incomprehensible theological question. Rumi described it as, "... setting my thoughts on fire." This is what set him firmly on the path of unlocking the inner secrets of the soul. Can you think of a similar situation in which you felt suddenly aware of something new for the first time?

There is no shortage of answers to these questions. Every religion, every philosopher, every self-help guru, and even the guy down the street all offer you advice. This preponderance of self-affirmation messages should be all the proof you need that human beings need meaning in their lives. We thrive on it; we cannot survive without it. Therefore, it wouldn't be too much of a stretch to say that there is a component within each of us that is attuned to awakening some sort of inner wellspring of hope and satisfaction. We were born to shine, but we each must learn how to polish ourselves. Rumi exhorts us to listen to our inner need, as opposed to our surface desires, and take that path at all costs.

> Go and seek true love, if you would let your spirit live; otherwise, you'll just be a slave to the passage of time.
>
> Don't look at yourself and think you're ugly or beautiful; only think upon love and what you seek.
>
> Don't look at yourself and think you're rotten or too ill (to make the journey); look upon your hope, O noble one.
>
> It matters not what condition you're in; keep searching. O you with the parched lip, keep searching for the water, for that parched lip of yours is the proof that one day you'll reach the gushing spring.
>
> A dry lip is merely a message sent to you by the water, telling you that your discomfort will eventually bring you to it some day.

Mathnawi III, 1436–1441

Let Rumi Be Your Guide

The Muslim religion that Rumi followed carries the strong message that we all must awaken our inner spirit in order to achieve contentment, meaning, and a purposeful life. All other major religions teach their followers to adopt this quest, as well. In this, there is a sign that all religions came from the same essential source, and Rumi recognized as much when he wrote the following:

> The many prayers and blessings that are invoked upon the righteous bring together in unison the praises of all the prophets. These invocations mingle together, like many jugs being emptied into a single pool.
>
> Given that the (Divine) object of all praise is not more than one being Himself, from this point of view, then, all religions are only one religion.
>
> Know then that every type of praise goes up to the Light of God, and is merely on loan to material objects and people.
>
> How can anyone praise any other besides Him, when only He has the right (to be praised)? Some go off in error due to their whims (and forget this truth).
>
> The Light of God compared with the natural world is like moonlight shining upon a wall at night—the wall is merely the focus for all those splendors.
>
> *Mathnawi* III, 2122–2127

Rumi's References _____

Rumi often alludes to the Light of God. This is a common metaphor throughout the works of many Muslim poets and mystics, and it goes back to a passage of the Qur'an that reads as follows: "God is the Light of the heavens and the earth. The example of His Light is like a nook. Within that nook is a lamp, and the lamp is encased in glass. The glass resembles a star, glittering (like a pearl) whose flame is lit from a blessed tree—an olive tree—neither from the East nor the West, whose oil is glistening and glowing, even before it's been lit! *Light upon Light!* God guides whomever He wants toward His Light, and this is how God gives examples to people, for God knows about all things."

—Qur'an (24:35)

The search for light in one's inner being is open to all people of all faiths, even those lacking in that department, for regardless of what a person holds dear, all human beings share the same essential human spirit. Now Rumi took this quest for inner meaning to its deepest levels. His expertise provides a whole host of shortcuts for us in our own struggle to be free of the earthly limitations that assail us. Again, this is a journey that all people from all backgrounds can embark upon, and what's more, Rumi has generously offered to be our guide. In these words, he tells us why:

> Whoever begins a journey without a leader, then every two days' worth of traveling becomes like a hundred years.
>
> Whoever rushes toward the holy shrine without a guide becomes as uncouth as the lot of confused men.
>
> Whoever starts a profession without having first learned from a teacher becomes the object of ridicule in his own town and nation.
>
> Except for maybe a single instance between the east and west, has any descendant of Adam ever stuck his head out (at birth) without parents?
>
> The one who gains is the one who earned; it's an unusual occurrence that someone should stumble upon buried treasure!
>
> *Mathnawi* III, 588–592

For Rumi, realization begins with an examination of the self. Without a critical look into our own inner nature, we cannot know or understand how to begin the journey toward self-actualization. So now, let us take Rumi as our guide and let his wisdom cascade over our senses. As we pass through the gardens of his poetry, try to glimpse the lessons that his words offer to us. Contemplate deeply—meditate—on the meanings of what they contain and draw out the lessons that can transform your life and bring you a new reason to feel joy and happiness. Take these gems of wisdom and don't hesitate—you have nothing to lose but all those things that have held you back from awakening the beauty within your soul!

Embrace Your Inner "You"

When you fall asleep, you leave your conscious state and enter upon your true self. You hear your inner voice speaking, and you think someone else spoke to you secretly in your dreams!

In the same way, there isn't just one small "you," my good friend. No way! You're the combination of both the sky and the deep sea!

The bigger "You" is magnified 900 times, like an ocean, within which 100 little "you"s can drown.

Really now, what use is there in saying either wakefulness or sleep? Be silent, for God knows the truth!

Mathnawi III, 1300–1304

There is a hidden world in your mind. When you look in the mirror, you see a reflection of reality, yet you would never say the reflection *is* the reality. In the same way, your conscious thoughts are but a reflection of a deeper ocean of being that makes up your totality. But just as people see our faces and make the faulty assumption that they know all about us, we, too, think our surface thoughts and fleeting desires are all we are. The mystery behind the face, the depth underneath the surface of the water—this is what's been hidden for too long. Rumi would have you stick your finger in that pool of your self-image, ripple the water, upset it, and then realize it is the mask hiding something far more significant. You can never dive in to the water and snatch a pearl until you accept that there is more to you than you originally thought.

The Stark Truth

Know that Hope is a deaf man who's heard about our impending death; yet, he's never heard of his own death or paid attention to his own illness.

Greed is a blind man: he sees shortcomings in others, no matter how small, and he spreads the news on every street corner. Even still, his blind eyes never see one speck of fault within himself, even though he's so skilled at finding fault! A naked man becomes afraid of losing his own pants; yet, how can anyone take a naked man's pants?

The materialistic person is stricken with poverty and fear; even though he has nothing, he lives in fear of thieves. He came into this world with nothing, and he'll leave it with nothing; yet, he's plagued with constant fear of being robbed!

When the moment of death arrives, and a chorus of wailing wells up by his side, his soul will laugh at its own fear. For in that instant, the rich person will realize he has no gold; the clever person will know he has no more schemes.

It's the same as when a child has a lap full of pretty shapes—he trembles for them like a rich man with his gold. If you take a piece away, then he starts to cry; if you give it back, he starts to laugh. Since the child is not swaddled in knowledge, neither his laughing nor his tears mean anything.

Mathnawi III, 2628–2639

Why is hope described as a deaf man? Because even in the face of the worst hardship or looming disasters, the human being can always cling to hope. It's our constant companion, and it's not scared off by loud noises. Why is greed described as a blind man? Because greed sees nothing good but itself, and it wants nothing for anyone but what will help itself. These two forces do combat in our minds. Sometimes, greed seems to overpower our sense of justice and our lives become that much more empty. No matter how much material wealth we acquire, we're in constant fear of ruin. Other times, our inner sense of goodness comes out on top, and the lifting of greed's oppression lets a ray of light shine within our souls. This adds strength to our reservoir of hope. Knowledge is the key to locking greed away and freeing hope from its dark prison.

> ### Footprints of the Master
> Sufi teachings are passed on from master to disciple in the form of instructive stories, coupled with meditative "endurance tests" involving chanting, seclusion, prayer, and other similar practices.

Seek the Opened Heart

There is many a one whose eye is awake, yet whose heart is asleep. In the end, what can creatures made of water and clay ever see?

The one who keeps his heart awake, though the eye of his head yet sleeps—such a heart will open 100 eyes!

If you're not in possession of an opened heart yet, then remain awake in study throughout the night. Look for that heart that can open, and struggle against your earthly desires.

If your heart is always awake, then rest in peace, for your inner eye is never dimmed from seeing the world around it.

The description of an awakened heart, O spiritual being, could not be accomplished even in thousands of verses!

Mathnawi III, 1222–1225, 1228

People are often hasty in their expectations. Our modern world compounds this phenomenon with fast food, fast cars, and high-speed you-name-it. Could it all be another deception of the world? Is it possible that our lonely hearts want everything to move faster and faster so we'll be too distracted to think about our approaching deadline of death, and thus we can avoid taking a hard look at our inner self?

The journey is a worthwhile one. If we don't feel "enlightened" after 20 minutes, it doesn't mean it's not possible; it doesn't mean we can never achieve it. It just means that the illusion of "quickness" needs to be laid to rest in our minds. Nothing worthwhile comes quickly. The payoff, however, is beyond what words can describe. Don't be afraid to learn new things on this journey and don't be daunted by patience. If you're not there yet, remain a student of the ways that will get you there. Learn to read books that challenge your soul, attend lectures and seminars, devote quiet time to yourself in your routines, and join the company of like-minded people. If Rome wasn't built in a day, surely your life won't be changed in an hour, but you can at least keep making the bricks!

> **Rumi's References**
>
> *Sabr* is the word Sufis use to describe patient perseverance. Without patience, Sufis believe people stand little chance to know themselves.

Why the Seeker Achieves the Goal

On the bank of a stream, there was a high wall. Sitting on top of that high wall was a very sad, thirsty man.

The wall prevented him from reaching the water; he was filled with longing for the water, like a fish might be if it were in the same situation.

Suddenly, he threw a loose brick down from the wall and it fell into the water. The noise of the splashing water echoed in his ears like words—words spoken by a dear and delicious friend.

The noise of the water made him feel intoxicated, as if he had drunk wine. The splashing sounds made by the water made that hard-pressed man feel better; then he began to tear off more bricks and throw them down from that place.

The water, however, made whimpering noises and said, "Hey you! What do you hope to gain by throwing bricks at me?"

The thirsty man replied, "O Water! I'm getting two things, and because of it I'll never stop what I'm doing. The first thing I'm getting is the splashing sounds of the water, which to a thirsty man sounds like a violin. The second thing is that, for every brick I tear off this wall, I come closer to you."

Mathnawi II, 1192–1199, 1206

Sometimes people realize that they're missing something in their lives, yet they hesitate to take the path of acquiring it. They remain in their state of emptiness, perhaps assailed by self-doubts, fear, or a feeling of unworthiness. At other times, they may feel that the journey will be too hard, too fraught with possible disappointment, or too complex to achieve. The phrase, "You can do anything you want" slips easily enough from the tongue, and this is the most common advice we hear; yet, when it comes time to starting any journey, we quickly become aware of how long the road will be.

Many get discouraged early on and choose not to take the road that leads to their desire, preferring to linger within the dream of hazy possibility, safe from the fear of disappointment. But what if the journey could be whittled down? What if we took it in little steps, and let every step be a mini-fulfillment? Any disappointment that arises would be measured against dozens of successes, so why would anyone quit when she's making such huge gains to offset any small losses? Eventually, the seeker will reach her goal, and she'll have had 1,000 little successes along the way to celebrate! So don't be afraid to start an endeavor. If you know what you want, just take it one step at a time, like a baby learning to walk. Complete each step in increments, as Rumi suggests, for each will give you the inspiration to take the next. Eventually, you'll reach whatever it is that will slake your dry thirst.

Consider Yourself a Treasure

Even if you were a powerful king who possessed every fortune, remember still that real fortune is something else, besides you.

One day your worldly fortune will disappear, and you'll be left with nothing, like a pauper. Let your soul be your fortune, O chosen one.

When you are your own fortune, O person of truth, then how can you, who are fortune personified, ever lose yourself?

How can you lose yourself, O person of goodness, when your very essence has become your kingdom and your treasure?

Mathnawi IV, 1109–1112

Most people, at some point in their lives, realize the futility of possessions. For a time, most people take the act of acquiring things as their reason to live; they wake up every morning with the goal to gather more "things" for themselves. When our expensive acquisitions, which provide us with only passing pleasures and momentary distractions, start to reveal how stingy we are with our inner selves, then we begin to feel dissatisfied with material things as a whole. Those who remain stuck in the material trap are among the most miserable of all. Those who break free of it are ready to find the fulfillment of all their deepest desires. When we drape ourselves in things, we merely get buried under a pile of trash. When we shed the love of things, we can finally understand that the most valuable treasure of all was within our own selves all along. Make your heart and soul your treasure, and spare no expense or effort in polishing that gemstone, for its luster will never fade, and its value will never decrease.

Putting It All Together

Awakening inner essence requires a certain amount of comparisons to be made between you, your material goals, and your short life span—which is most important of the three. Until a person finally gets a sense of alarm that his short life might slip away before he ever has the chance to make sense of it all in his deepest level of consciousness, then he'll make no progress in gaining inner tranquility and peace. An easy way to give yourself a jumpstart, and perspective, on this whole process is first to look at the average life span of a male or female—it's around 75 to 80 years, give or take a few years. Then subtract the amount of years you've already lived. Next, add that number to what year it is today. That will be your approximate "exit date" from this world. Write that number on a piece of paper and stick it some place where you'll notice it often. That's one deadline you cannot avoid, and that constant reminder will surely keep you focused on the quest for meaning in this world! Rumi begs you to realize that there's more to you than meets the eye, and he cautions you that there's no time to lose in your quest. The only life that should be pitied is the life of a living robot, who was born, worked for a time, and then died, without ever knowing why.

The Least You Need to Know

◆ Life has a way of drowning our sense of awareness under a flood of distractions.

◆ Rumi believed that because life was short, a person should devote more time to exploring her inner self, rather than immersing one's self too much in materialism.

◆ Rumi held that a novice should seek the benefit of a spiritual guide to help him avoid frustration and pitfalls.

◆ According to Rumi, a life lived without getting in touch with one's true self is a living hell resulting in bitterness and sorrow.

Chapter 5

Igniting the Divine Spark

In This Chapter

◆ Discovering in Rumi's *Fihi Ma Fihi* the real importance of your life's work in comparison to the awakening of your soul

◆ Exploring various techniques of motivation to propel you on the path of self-discovery

◆ Learning how to direct your essential nature toward goodness and faith

◆ Gaining useful insight and understanding to help sustain you in your everyday life

Once you've accepted that uncovering the *real* you is of the utmost priority, the next logical step is to begin that journey of self-discovery. One may ask, "How do I get started? What do I need to do? Will it be a lot of work?" Be careful not to get too caught up in questions like this, as sometimes it's our overemphasis on initial preparation that actually stalls our progress. Our desire to lay out a plan and to get everything "right" before we begin the journey is a kind of distraction in itself. As with anything else, actually embarking on the journey is usually the hardest part of the whole endeavor. So why don't we get right to it and bypass the planning and inquiries altogether.

You already know that there's a vibrant spark deep down within the recesses of your soul. You've felt it sometimes, even as at other times you've forgotten it. Therefore, the real question is not how to recognize your soul's presence (because you know it's there) but, rather, how to stoke the embers of your already warm spirit until it glows with an increasingly bright ambiance. How do you fan that little flame inside so that it becomes hot enough to burn through that shell that's been encasing your spirit for so long? How do you maintain the glow against any chill wind of uncertainty, self-doubt, or fatigue that may try to dim the light? Are there ways to keep the motivation alive in tough times? Are there any techniques that can help you through the long dry spells of impatience? These are some of the questions that we'll explore in this chapter, and as always, Rumi will be right there to answer all of our concerns.

And What Is Our Purpose Again?

On the subject of human purpose, in the fourth chapter of his collected discourses, otherwise known as *Fihi Ma Fihi*, Rumi has this to say:

> There's one thing in this world that must never be neglected. Even if you forget to do everything else in this life, as long as you fulfill that one main task, you won't have anything to worry about. On the other hand, even if you manage to accomplish everything else there is to do in your life, leaving nothing undone, if you neglect that one single task, then it will be as if you accomplished nothing at all.
>
> It's the same as if a king sent you out into the countryside to perform a specific job. Now let's say you go and complete a hundred other tasks along the way, but you fail to do that one particular thing—the job for which you were sent out in the first place. In the eyes of the king, it would be as if you had achieved nothing. In the same way, we human beings have come into this world for a

particular purpose, and that one purpose is what we were specifically created for. If we don't accomplish it, then despite whatever else we may do, we will, in reality, have done nothing at all.

What is this one specific task for which we human beings were created? Rumi next quotes a verse from the Qur'an that says this:

> We offered the responsibility (of self-awareness) to the heavens, the earth, and the mountains, but they all refused to accept it out of fear (of the consequences). Humanity agreed to undertake it, though it overstepped and was foolish. (33:73)

Rumi's References

The teachings of the Qur'an form the basis of Rumi's *Mathnawi*. When he's not quoting from the Qur'an directly, he's weaving stories and parables that mimic some aspect of the Qur'an or another. This is why the *Mathnawi* is called "the Qur'an in Persian."

The implication of this verse is that out of all creation, only we human beings have an expansive soul and are, by design, naturally conscious of the impact of our actions. Thus, we have a grave responsibility upon our shoulders to use that power wisely. To misuse these gifts is to be ungrateful, despite whatever other achievements we may successfully complete. Therefore, our single-most important task is to open our souls to God. By doing this we become aware of the full depth of our special gifts, we learn to shrug off the call of the material world, and we become motivated to do right and good by our fellow creatures—and ourselves. This is what God intended for us in His giving us a soul to begin with. Rumi continues his discourse here:

> Perhaps you might say, "Even if I don't accomplish that one task, yet still I've completed so many other things." Well, you weren't created for those other things. It's like being given a sword of priceless Indian steel, the like of which can only be found in the treasuries of kings, and then using it as a butcher's knife for slicing rotten meat, saying, "I'm not letting this sword go to waste. I'm putting it to so many good uses." How pitiful and ridiculous is that! God the Most High has given you a higher value than you

realize, for He said, "God has bought from the faithful their lives and their possessions, and in exchange He will grant them the gift of Paradise."

Thus, an eternal paradise of reunion with the Divine is in store for those who hearken to the call of their thirsty souls. Rumi continues his argument with this poignant quote:

> A poet said, "You're more precious than both the heavens and the earth. What more can I say? You don't even know what you're worth."

Therefore, as we begin our journey we can steel our resolve with the realization that we have intrinsic value in our very being—it's not in what we do, what we make, who we know, etc. This makes it easier to accept that we have a responsibility to our deepest self, to awaken it, polish it, and let it be the lens through which we see the world and life within it. Worldly accomplishments are fine, but we mustn't forget to fulfill the one task for which we've been created: to awaken our souls to our ultimate potential. And so, without any preparation we've already embarked on the journey by realizing this one fact! Here is what Rumi comments:

> What's inside a fruit is better than what's on the outside. Likewise, think of your body as a mere shell, while its inner essence is your real friend. That's just it: human beings have a valuable inner nature. Look for that alone, if you're truly among those (inspired by) the breath (of God).

Mathnawi III, 3417–3418

Rumi is shown here with students in this fifteenth-century Persian painting. His arms are raised as he chants and rotates in mediation.

What Excuse Do You Have?

Rumi lays out the following proposition clearly: you have value, and the only way you can fully realize that value is if you accept that you were given a soul for a purpose. To do anything less than polish it and set it free is a lost opportunity at experiencing real life. Who would be so foolish as to turn down a treasure, once he or she knows it was there? Here is what Rumi wrote:

> The lovely moon shone upon me last night.

> "Leave me now," I said, "for I'll not see you tonight." As she left, I heard her say, "Well done, O moody one. You won't even open your door when a treasure comes."

> From the *Divan*

Footprints of the Master

Rumi had many female students and disciples. They attended his lectures, were teachers to others, and would also participate in the whirling meditation sessions he led. The most famous of Rumi's female acolytes was Fakhr un-Nisa', who was known as the "Rab'iah" in her day. (Rabi'ah al-Adawiyya, who passed away in 801, is perhaps the most famous female Muslim mystic in history.)

Of what value are all of our accomplishments, if we leave this life without ever having a deeper understanding of who we are and our place in the universe? How could we turn down such a treasure when it offers itself to us? For Rumi, there is neither excuse nor justification for not getting in touch with the gem that lies buried under your exterior. He says this in his fourth discourse:

> Perhaps you'll offer an excuse, saying, "I'm devoting myself to more important things. I'm studying law, philosophy, logic, astronomy, medicine, and all the rest." Well, for whose sake but your own are you doing all these things? If it's the study of law, you're only pursuing it so no one can cheat you out of a loaf of bread or strip you of your clothes or kill you. In other words, it's for your own peace of mind, and so on with all the other areas of study. All these things are connected with your own situation and serve only your own goals.

Know that for you there's another kind of sustenance and security to sustain you that's far better than this ration of physical sleeping and eating. The Prophet once said, "I spend the night in the presence of my Lord. He's the One Who gives me my sustenance." But look! In the life of this world, you've forgotten all about your heavenly food, being so preoccupied as you are with material provisions. Throughout the night and the day, you're busy feeding the needs of your physical body. However, this body is like your horse, and the life of this world is its stable.

What the horse eats is not what the rider eats. The rider has his own kind of rest, food, and pleasure. Yet, because the animalistic body and the instinctual urges within you have the upper hand over you, you've tarried with your horse in the stable, and you've not let yourself live in the home of kings and princes in the eternal realm. Your heart wants to be there, but because the body has the upper hand, you're subject to the body's control and you remain its prisoner.

Thus, as Rumi explains it, within our busy lives we must not forget where our true purpose lies. The never-ending race to get more "stuff" in our short lives leaves our spirit starving at the end of the day. All other pursuits pale in comparison to our real need—that of nourishing our heart and soul. We are spiritual beings with a relationship to something greater than ourselves. Regardless of the faith, or lack thereof, all people are endowed with an inner depth that must be experienced and expanded upon in order to realize what being truly human is. To leave the key to the treasury lying in the dust before the door is to be ungrateful for the gifts waiting to be unleashed within. We must hurry, however, for there is little time to lose. Our life span is short and when we finally realize what we must do, the constant ticking of the clock must be our companion and reminder. This is what Rumi intoned:

> You're joined to a life that lasts for but a day, so much so that you can't stand any mention of death.
>
> Life may look like a home, but it's really a home that ends in decay. You would realize this; yet, your donkey *has fallen asleep on the way!*
>
> From the *Divan*

The Spirit Responds to the Call

One need not worry or fret about any secret magic to begin to unlock her inner soul. It will respond to the one who seeks it. Rumi said as much when he wrote this:

> Whatever grows on the earth is grown for the sake of those in need. This is so the seeker can find what he's looking for. If God created the heavens above, He did so for the sake of meeting needs.
>
> Where there is pain, that's where the cure goes. Where there is poverty, that's where the rations go. Where there are difficult questions, that's where the answers go, and where there is a ship, that's where the water goes.
>
> Don't worry about looking for the water; get thirsty so that the water will rush to you from above and below. Unless the precious child is born, how can milk begin to flow from the breast?
>
> Go and run through these hills and meadows so you can get really thirsty; let yourself succumb to the heat! After a while, you'll hear the noise of approaching thunder, and soon you'll hear the sounds of water in the stream, O you who would be king!

Mathnawi III, 3208–3215

Rumi's References

Rumi often ended important sections of verses in the *Mathnawi* with the simple command of *khamush,* or silence. This was his way of telling the readers to open their inner voice, and turn off their tongue for a while so they can reflect on what they've learned.

In other words, your desire is enough to get the process started. Sure, you will need determination and patience along the way to achieve greater levels of insight, but your thirst will help sustain you in that quest. When Rumi mentions running through "these" hills and meadows to build a raging thirst, he's giving us a metaphor: keep on this path; study, think, and pray, for exerting yourself in these kinds of activities is really a way of building up your desire to know yourself on an even deeper level! Rumi encourages us with the following words.

Whether he be slow or quick (on the chase), the seeker is the one who shall find. As you search, use both your hands in your endeavor, for the quality of a searcher is an excellent guide along the way.

Whether you're lame or limping, bent over or deformed, never cease to crawl toward Him; never give up your search for Him! Sometimes with words, sometimes with silence, or maybe by smell, notice in every place the scent of the King.

Mathnawi III, 978–981

Rumi's Words of Advice

Now let us take a journey through some of Rumi's words of advice to gain a sense of what kinds of practices and understandings we can acquire to help our progress along the way. His counsel is essential, time-tested, and sincere for those who learn to meditate on the deeper meaning of their lives and ignite the divine spark.

You Don't Need Any Special Skills

Even though you have no equipment, keep searching nonetheless, for equipment isn't necessary on the path to the Lord.

Whenever you see someone already involved in the search, O child, become his friend and devote yourself to him completely.

When you become the neighbor of a seeker, you yourself will be a seeker, too! In the shadow of a conqueror, you shall become a conqueror, as well.

If an ant wants to become as strong as Solomon, don't laugh at it for its goals.

Think of everything you ever gained in treasure and skill—wasn't there a time when it was all just a dream and a quest?

Mathnawi III, 1445–1449

There are two main points here that Rumi offers. The first point goes back to something discussed in Chapter 2, that people should seek out the company of like-minded individuals who help encourage their spiritual studies. Think of it like arranging a workout companion: if you can't get that extra mile in on the treadmill, your friend will cajole you into reaching that next milestone. The second main point is that there should be no shame in being a beginner or in having a lofty goal. What is life but dreams of the future? There isn't a single powerful person alive who didn't start out as a penniless dreamer. Therefore, your dreams are just as valid as anyone else's.

Let Yourself Be Open-Minded

> Would anyone write something on a paper that's already been used? Would anyone plant a tree where one has already been planted? Of course not! He would look for blank paper on which to write or a vacant lot in which to plant.
>
> So why don't you, O companion, become a vacant lot or a blank paper, so you can be made splendid by *the pen of revelation*, and so the Most Merciful can plant a seed within you?
>
> *Mathnawi* V, 1961–1964

Rigidity is the most serious impediment to progress in nearly every human endeavor. Think of all the human suffering that has come about through the ages from the individual to collective level, simply because people refused to be open-minded. Think of how many compromises you've made because they were better alternatives than standing your ground at that moment.

An ancient Chinese proverb points out that trees that bend in the wind will survive, while those that remain rigid will snap. Our souls are the same way. If you are to know yourself on a deeper level, you have to be willing to put your assumptions into a wider perspective. You must not cling to an idea whose time you know has passed. Be willing to consider new ideas, for that's the only way people grow. Put some of your old beliefs and attitudes on notice that if they don't start to work with you, then they'll be left on the curbside. By doing so you are preparing the soil so something beautiful can take root, and laying a blank page on the table so a greater Hand than yours can begin to write the story of your life.

Have You Inspected Yourself Lately?

You know how much every item costs; yet, if you don't know how much you're worth, then it's all for nothing.

You know all about your lucky and unlucky stars, yet, you never consider if you're lucky or unlucky yourself!

That's it! That's the heart of all knowledge; knowing how you're going to fare on the day when an account will be made of you!

You know exactly what your beliefs require of you, but have you looked at what your own foundation is, to see whether it's good or not?

(Getting a sense) of your own foundation is better for you than (following) the two core principles (of your faith), for in that way you can finally get a handle on your own basic nature, O you who would be great.

Mathnawi III, 2652–2656

One of Rumi's overriding themes is that each person must be willing to take a good look at herself and measure who she is and what she really stands for. In other words, a person may say, "I'm this or that," but what is she really all about, deep down? Even though the age-old adage—*know thyself*—may sound easy, most people never undertake such a personal accounting. Whether from fear of finding shortcomings within, being distracted from our busy lives, or from never having really thought about the inner self and its well-being, the pitfalls that hold us back are many and not always easy to recognize, but it is a journey worth taking.

So how is it done? How does a person begin to peel away his façade and peek into his hidden foundation? Initially it's by learning to ask yourself questions about your actions and motivations. At least a few times a day, ask yourself about how you interacted with others, including the following:

◆ What did you say?

◆ How did you respond to the various situations you encountered?

◆ Are you satisfied with what you did?

- What could you have done better?

- Have you learned anything?

- Do you regret anything?

- What did you really want to do and why?

- How are you feeling right now and why?

- Is there anything you want or need to revisit and change today and why?

- What urges have you felt and what do you think they mean?

Write these questions down, along with others you think would be helpful, and tack them up somewhere. Make it a daily habit to carry on a dialogue with the one person you (should) know best and who you can (and should) be most honest with. Remember, too, that this type of self-examination is not a one-time thing. Would you look in the mirror one morning, be satisfied with your appearance, and then never look in the mirror again for the rest of the day or month, assuming you still looked good every day? I didn't think so! People constantly check and recheck their outer appearance, especially when they think no one is looking. Do you know where I'm going with this? That you also need to look at your inner appearance—your behavior, attitude, feelings, and concerns— at different points throughout the day, too, just like you check out your hair and teeth.

 Wisdom of the Ages

Rumi wrote, "Expel greed, jealousy, and hatred from your heart. Evil thoughts and anger— learn to let them go. Deny this and you'll lose, so cut your losses now. Own this and your profits will quickly grow." —From the *Divan*

We already use our brains to discuss our daily lives, albeit in a semi-conscious sort of way. Now we just need to harness our thoughts on a more deliberate, contemplative, and active level. We have to begin to notice what happens with our life more consciously. Do this by rehashing events in your mind that occurred earlier in the day. Small things, large things, odd things—they all have a lesson to teach. Reflection is the key that opens the door to self-awareness.

Perhaps you had a conversation with someone—pick it apart. Maybe you noticed a butterfly and were temporarily taken with its beauty—reflect on why you felt this way. Maybe you made a mistake—think about how you could have avoided it. Maybe something alarmed you or made you angry—why? As Rumi advised, doing this kind of self-reflection vis-à-vis your thoughts, actions, and interactions is the only way you'll be able to get a handle on your spirit. Try it, build up to more frequent self-reflection, then practice some more. Soon you'll feel more presence of mind in everything you do. Rumi wrote of the phenomenon of growing awareness in these words:

> Looking up (from the darkness of your mundane existence) will give you a light to see by, though your eyes may become dazzled by the bright sky at first—oh, indeed they will!

> Let your eyes become accustomed to the light, and as long as you're not a bat, then keep looking up in that direction.

> When you can see the ultimate end of things, it means you're looking with the light. Focusing on the whim of the moment is nothing more than a dark grave.

> *Mathnawi* II, 1975–1977

Look into the Self

Rumi was a strong proponent of self-inspection and reflection. Without it, it would be impossible for our ailment to be diagnosed and a cure prescribed. Listen to the manner in which Rumi asks us to approach our own self:

> The body is like a letter: look into it and see—is it worthy of being read by the King? Take it. Go into a corner; open the letter; read it. Are its words such as a king would approve? If it's not good enough, then tear it to pieces; write another letter and fix what was wrong.

> But don't think that the body can so easily be opened like a letter. If that were so, then everyone would see the secrets that the heart contains. Oh, how hard that letter is to open! It's a job for grown-ups, not for children playing around.

We're all too readily satisfied after reading the table of contents. That's because we're all sunk in selfishness and foolish desires. The table of contents is a trap for the rude, who think the rest of the scroll is the same as that.

Now look at the title page—don't look away from it—and God knows the best way for you to change. The title of your life is like a statement from your tongue. Now look into the text of your scroll, especially into the heart, to see if it matches up with what you say, so your actions won't be laced with hypocrisy.

Really now, when you're carrying a heavy bag, you have to see what's inside it! What's sour in it? What's sweet? What's worth carrying along with you?

Empty your bag of the worthless stones within, and save yourself from wasted effort and disgrace. Fill the sack only with the treasures you would bring to nobles and kings.

Mathnawi IV, 1564–1577

Rumi's References

One of the most influential books of mystical poetry in Rumi's young adulthood was called *The Conference of the Birds*, written by Fariduddin 'Attar (d. 1220). This book concerned the journey of a host of birds who wanted to find their true king. When they set out on their travels, the birds took a majestic and wise bird as their guide. Along the way, through the use of examples, parables, and stories, the guide helped the birds to understand that their goals for self-fulfillment rested not on reaching a specific destination, but on purifying their inner selves. This is a constant theme in Rumi's work, as well.

Sometimes, or oftentimes, we consider who we really are in terms of how we measure up to the expectations of others, and wonder, and worry, if we're really worthy in the eyes of our peers. This is a path littered with traps and snares for the unwary. When we look to others for approval, fears and self-doubts often plague our mind and bring down our spirit—oh, the little voices constantly telling us we're not good enough!

But what are we measuring ourselves against? Too often, we haven't a clue and we unfairly rely upon vague whispers of "he said" and "she said"! Of course, this keeps the vicious circle of inadequacy going, and we may never feel we measure up. But what if we clearly defined who we want to judge us? What if we stopped for a moment and considered whose opinions really matter? For Rumi, he only cared what God thought about him. That was the beginning and the end of his self-examination. The opinions of people should not be the focus we strive for when we examine our self and worth. Who are we to give other human beings so much power over our own peace of mind? Take back from others the power to pass judgment over you.

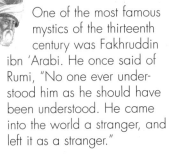

Wisdom of the Ages

One of the most famous mystics of the thirteenth century was Fakhruddin ibn 'Arabi. He once said of Rumi, "No one ever understood him as he should have been understood. He came into the world a stranger, and left it as a stranger."

We can apply the same principle at every level in our own lives. Never say, "I don't know how he feels about me." Rather you should first ask, "Is that person worthy of my concern?" Only after you've determined that to be so, then should you say, "Am I the kind of person who is worthy of his company?" Also, take a look at your inner components—your habits, your likes, your interests, and such—and determine if they're really worth lugging with you any longer in this life. When your thoughts are focused, then you can decide if so-and-so is worth your attention and devotion and you will know how to mold yourself into who you really want to be.

Is a Seeker Expected to Be Perfect?

Unlike any other endeavor, there are no exams to take to judge how much your soul has awakened. You need not worry about the amount of mistakes you've accumulated, or the setbacks you've experienced. If you've lapsed into some old habits that were harmful to you or inadvertently forgot to examine yourself for a while, there will be no taskmaster there to chastise you (other than yourself). All your efforts, great or small, and all your trials and setbacks in life are all a part of the quest.

Sufi literature, along with a large part of the literature found in most other religions, is full of stories of people who lost their way or stumbled, only to find their way to complete satisfaction in the end. There are no moments where you have to feel like a failure, for there is no chance to fail yourself as long as you're thirsty for some kind of progress. Even a life filled with hardship can be a blessing that will open your heart to what you seek. On this journey, failure in life is nothing more than a chance at self-improvement! Here's what Rumi wrote:

> Who is drawing you nearer, O questioner? The One Who forbids you to say anything! You make 100 vows to go somewhere, yet He leads you somewhere else.

> He turns your reins in every direction so that the untrained horse can realize he has a rider on his back. The clever horse will pace himself evenly, because he knows a rider is directing his way.

> He's set your heart on 100 cherished goals; then He disappoints you and breaks your heart. Even as He broke the wings of your first desire, how could you not have known that a wing-breaker was there? Since it was His order that snapped the cord of so many of your plans, how could you not have realized the power of God's command?

> However, as time goes by, some of your resolutions and goals are achieved, so that you can gain a sense of hope that your plans might possibly succeed, even as He may destroy some of your intentions once more.

> If He never let you taste success, then your heart would be in constant despair. How could you ever have any expectations of success then? Unless the kernel of expectation can be implanted in the heart, how can a barren soul ever realize its dependence on the divine command?

> Through failure, those who would love are made aware of their Lord. Failure is the guide to eternal bliss. Listen, O noble one, to the tradition, "Paradise is surrounded by hardships and tests."

> If everything you do ends in failure, know that there is Someone whose pleasure is fulfilled. The sincere have become broken before Him, yet how does this compare to those who love Him?

Wisdom of the Ages

Rumi once described his newfound wisdom in these words, "I was once dead; I came alive. I started to laugh; the power of love arrived, making me forever powerful inside. My eye is peaceful now; my soul has become brave; I now have the heart of lion, even as like Venus I shine."

—From the *Divan*

The intelligent are brought down before Him because they have to be, while those who love Him are brought down willingly 100 times.

The intelligent are His slaves, while those who love Him are like candy to Him. "Come against your will" is the motivation of the intelligent, while "Come of your own free will" is the blossoming spring of those who have lost their hearts.

Mathnawi III, 4455–4472

Indeed, we must realize that hope can never truly die, no matter how many setbacks or hard days we have, for occasionally, things do work out. Therefore, difficult times are really opportunities for us to practice patience and perseverance. Likewise, every amount of progress, no matter how small, is like a treasure, for it keeps the engine of our hope alive, even if it sometimes seems so distant. We have to realize that the cycle of hope and failure is the overseer of patience, and that God dashes our plans only to teach us to open our hearts ever wider to divine destiny. What seems to be bad luck is really a way for you to explore your soul even more deeply. Rumi explains the matter this way:

> Look at the chickpea floating in the pot, how it leaps when it's put under the fire. As it's being boiled, it keeps rising to the top; it cries out in 100 ways, saying, "Why are you scalding me with fire? Since you thought I was good enough to buy, why are you turning me upside down now?"

> The cook goes on hitting it with her ladle and says, "Come on now! Boil nicely; don't try to escape the one who made the fire. I'm not boiling you because I hate you, but rather so you can become tasty and flavorful, and gain good qualities and mingle with the spirit (of the soup). This pain that you're enduring now isn't because you're unloved. When you were young and fresh in the garden you drank in water. Your drinking of that water then was for the sake of burning in this fire now!"

God's mercy comes before His wrath, and part of His mercy is you being made to suffer from hardships. Through His wrath, (you learn to give up your foolish desires for this material world.) O Chickpea, keep on boiling in turmoil, so that neither your desire to exist nor your ego may remain a part of you.

Mathnawi III, 4159–4165, 4169, 4178

The Ultimate Pay-Off

Searching for greater awareness within one's self is like a never-ending payday. Through the years, life becomes sweeter, sorrow and hardship become balanced with the balm of understanding and deliberation, the fear of death fades away, and our every interaction becomes more meaningful and immediate. Other people also notice when a person rises from her inner slumber and pierces the veil of going through the motions of life. This sometimes makes them aware of their own inner deadness and puts the seed of desire within them, as well. Light upon light and beauty upon beauty emanate from those who learn to see with the eye of the spirit, rather than with the dull eye of the material body. Rumi apprised us of this very phenomenon in these words:

When God spoke to the rose, He made it laugh in beautiful splendor. When He spoke to my heart, He made it 100 times more beautiful.

Mathnawi III, 4129

The time to nourish the soul is always nigh. When the soul is ignited and the thirst for inner peace and satisfaction grows, then the real progress begins. Have you ever wondered at the beauty of certain people you have known or read about who were such farsighted and noble souls? Their spirit had a coming-out party. Yours wants one, too! Rumi describes the process like this:

The body is a slender home, and the soul inside is squished! (God) wrecked it so He could make a palace out of it.

I'm squished like a baby in the womb; I'm nine months old already; I have to come out! Unless my mother suffers from labor pains, (then how can I escape)? I'm burning up in this prison!

My mother, my physical nature, is being birthed through the pangs of death, so that the lamb (of my spirit) can be released from the (material body of the) ewe. Let the lamb graze in the green pastures now. Come then, open your womb, for this lamb has grown too big!

If the pain of childbirth is hard on the mother, well, for the baby it's a liberation. A pregnant woman cries out at childbirth, saying, "Where can I run?" But the baby comes out laughing and says, "Finally, I'm free!"

Mathnawi III, 3555–3561

The Least You Need to Know

◆ Our main purpose in this world is not to gain wealth or fame or to accomplish personal goals; rather it's to awaken our inner self and become aware of who we are as spiritual beings.

◆ There are no special skills required to ignite the quest for self-awareness. It does help to associate with like-minded individuals, however, for external support.

◆ Failure in life is a way to improve one's patience and to gain insight into the deeper lessons of life.

◆ Progress may be slow at times on the journey, but the thirst to achieve an expansive soul is quite enough to sustain the sincere seeker.

Chapter 6

Fighting the Illusion That Binds You

In This Chapter

◆ Learning how to recognize the many traps and snares of life that can blind your senses to the more important task of self-actualization

◆ Discovering ways in which you can combat materialism and lead a more spiritually satisfying life

◆ Exploring the nature and good offerings of this world and death without regrets

◆ Understanding Rumi's conception of life and how it differs from materialistic philosophies

There are many kinds of triumphs and failures in this world. If you traced the cause of each back to its source, you might be surprised to find that nearly all of them are rooted in our physical needs, wants, or desires. In other words, if you closely examined all the challenges, aggravations, joys, and sorrows found in the average person's life, you might find that the majority of those results have to do with the person's success (or lack thereof) in acquiring physical items or experiences—whether because the person can't do without them, or because he or she *really* wants to have them.

The more esoteric teachings found in every religion are oriented toward instructing people on how to live with less, not more. Of course, this flies in the face of conventional wisdom that says the more you acquire, the more successful a person you have become. Yet, when a person's daily needs are met, what will more possessions bring to the quality of his or her life? This is a wide issue, and Rumi wrote extensively on it. In this chapter, we'll explore some of what Rumi had to say about materialism and its dangers. In the end, you may find that you'll look upon your own possessions with a slightly different eye.

Peering Through the Looking Glass

While you're traveling on this journey toward awakening the inner self, you will soon notice that your awareness of life and its meaning are becoming enriched. This will, in turn, result in slight modifications to your daily life, interactions with others, and routines. It will be a voluntary evolution at every step of the way. As we begin to understand more, our satisfaction with our inner self will continue to increase, no matter what the actual circumstances are of the world we experience around us. Although you may have times of forgetfulness or bouts of busy distraction, the arc of progress will never seek to descend again. Rumi advanced this notion of perpetual progress when he said, "When the fire is lit inside, there's no putting it out." Rumi further offered inspiration to us as follows:

> (A seeker) will advance from level to level until he becomes discerning, wise, and capable. He will have no recollection of his former state of mind, for from this lower position of awareness there was a migration to be made so he could escape from the clutches of greed and self-centeredness; ultimately he will be able to see 100,000 shades of marvelous knowledge.

> He had fallen asleep and became forgetful of the past, yet how could he be left in that state of forgetfulness? From that slumber he will finally be brought back again to wakefulness. Then he can poke fun at himself in his new condition, saying, "What was all that stress I was suffering from when I was asleep? How could I

have forgotten the state of real understanding? How could I have not known that sadness and stress are the effects of being asleep (to reality), and that they're an illusion of the mind and a fantasy?"

Be that as it may, in this world, which is the dream of the sleeper, the sleeper feels that what he's experiencing is real, until the dawn of Death arrives and he's delivered from the darkness of conjecture and lies.

Mathnawi IV, 3647–3655

> **Footprints of the Master**
>
> There are three main practices that Sufis employ to gain deeper insight and spiritual discipline. These are known as *dhikr* (which is a kind of group chanting), *sama'* (which is moving meditation), and seclusion (which is forced isolation for contemplation).

Learning to See the Reality

One of the first tasks that you must perform on this path is to come to grips with the illusory nature of this world and the life it offers. Raise your hands before your eyes for a moment. You see skin, fingers, and perhaps some veins beneath the surface. But do your hands tell the whole story of your life? Do they convey the totality of who you are and what you stand for? You can perform tasks with your hands. You can pick up objects with them and create and break things at will. You can express both love and hate through your hands, and through them, the world is transformed on a daily basis.

But do your hands express their own reality? Yes, you might say, for you can physically see them before your own eyes. But do your hands actually contain love, creativity, power, or hate? No, those qualities lay elsewhere. So where do these things exist? In what part of your body are your love, creativity, anger, and whole host of other qualities and emotions? Are they physically in your heart? No, that's just a pump for your blood. Are they physically in your brain? Well, if your brain was removed and examined, could you find those things in there somewhere? Not really. A scientist can quantify chemicals and measure electrical impulses, yet the quality of consciousness or awareness is so much more than mere organic processes. Your totality, the depth of your consciousness, the inner recesses of the unique being that make up the individual "you" are beyond the physical and are entirely on another plane of existence altogether.

Wisdom of the Ages _____

Rumi wrote the following to describe our inability to notice our own transient nature: "The world is being renewed at every moment, even though we're unaware of it (due to the slow pace of change.) In the same way, just like a stream, life is also constantly being reborn, even though in the body it appears as if it's all part of the same thing." —*Mathnawi* I, 1144–1145

Similarly, this world is its own kind of illusion. If you think about it, success is not something that grows in the forest. Happiness cannot be bought at the store. Fulfillment doesn't happen when it rains. In other words, the world is a physical object. We ride upon it, raise its dust for a while, and then we leave it. By itself, it has no meaning other than the meaning we assign to it in our own minds. Thus, we are creatures devoted to assigning meaning to things. If we focus too closely on the forms and objects, such as our physical urges might suggest to us, then we'll be in danger of losing the bigger picture, where the ultimate meaning above our collective understanding exists. Rumi said this:

> In this sweet ocean of life, our physical forms are moving ever so fast, like cups on the surface of the water. We float like bowls on the sea for as long as we remain unfilled; however, when the bowl becomes full, it sinks beneath the waves.

> Reality is hidden; we only see the material world. (The movement of) our forms cause waves and splashing on the surface of the sea, and those shapes made by our forms are the vehicles we attempt to use to approach Reality, yet Reality pushes them far away.

> As long as the heart doesn't recognize the One Who gave it consciousness, as long as the arrow doesn't recognize the master archer who shot it, then the oblivious person will keep on thinking his horse is lost, even though he's sitting right on top of it as it runs along with him on the road.

That swell fellow thinks he's lost his horse, even though that horse has been flying along with him like the wind! In distress and curiosity, that unfocused soul rushes from door to door asking, "Where's my horse? Who took it from me?" Yet, the people reply, "What's that thing there under you, O sir?"

"Yes." he intones. "That's my horse, but where is *the* horse (that will carry me to my destination?)" O nimble rider in search of a horse, come to your senses! The soul is lost simply on account of its being so close!

With a belly full of water, how can you be so dry like an empty jar? How can you ever hope to see (the truth of the) reds, greens, and yellows unless you also see the undivided light (from which they came)? But since your focus was lost within all the colors (of the material world), those colors became a screen for you and kept you from noticing the (greater) Light (of Reality).

Then, with the onset of darkness, those colors ultimately became hidden from you. (Because of this, when you finally noticed the emptiness in your soul), you realized that your ability to see those (mundane) colors was a result of (the greater) Light. No individual colors can be seen without an external source of light; and so it is with the inner colors of the fantasy world.

Outer forms of light come from the sun and the stars, while inner light is a reflection of the rays of (God's) glory. The light that allows the eye to see is in truth the light of the heart.

The light of the eye is produced by the light of the heart. The light that illuminates the heart is from the Light of God, which is pristine and separate from the light of the mind and the senses.

def•i•ni•tion

The term for *light* (as in spiritual growth) used among Sufis is derived from the Arabic word **noor** (nūr), which means to be illuminated.

Mathnawi I, 1110–1127

The Truth of Our Achievements

As the ebb and flow of time passes, we human beings struggle to survive. We also place importance on our work and physical achievements. Yet, nothing we build or invent will last forever. Whatever fortune we amass will be dispersed and subsumed. Whatever children we bear will eventually pass on. We have the illusion of material progress in our own lives, even as we have the illusion of progress through the ages. Yet, no matter how far we rise (or think we rise), the earth eventually brings us all back down to dust. Our entire species is essentially ocean waves crashing on the shore of life one after another, only to recede and rejoin the ocean from whence they came. Rumi wrote this about it:

> By day and by night there is movement of foam on the sea. You can see the foam, but not the sea—how amazing! We bump into each other like boats in the night; our sight is dimmed, even though we're in clear water.
>
> You who've gone to sleep in the body's boat! You've seen the water (of your life all around you), yet look to the (real) Water that courses over (mundane earthly) water.
>
> The water (of your life) is driven by (a greater) Water, even as the spirit has (a greater) Spirit calling to it.
>
> *Mathnawi* III, 1272–1274

Human activity seems to move at the speed of light, yet for all our frantic activity, the defining moment of our lives is the moment of our death. That's where all of our individual achievement stops. We can lose ourselves in the blur of the group and take solace in the false belief that our busy lives and achievements will make death impossible. This is the same as falling asleep at the wheel and riding in a driverless, runaway car. This car will crash and damage us, unless—until—we come to our spiritual senses and gain awareness and reach for the bountiful life that lies far beyond the material.

Eternal Life Is Not Possible Here

A constant theme in both the *Divan* and *Mathnawi* is to learn the lesson of our transient nature in this life. Indeed, what greater teacher is there than our inevitable end? Like a man standing at the gallows, we all must take our turn. Yet, often the one at the end of the line foolishly thinks he's safe from it, even as he makes lofty plans with the people standing all around him. Rumi advised us to leap ahead into the future and see our own end before it comes, and also to see the end of all whom we love before it actually occurs. When we make that leap, then what cause will there be for any hate, anger, or envy to remain? This is what Rumi wrote:

> All men and women in this world are in a constant state of dying. Consider what they say as a father's final instructions to his son upon his deathbed. Understanding and pity will grow within your heart if you adopt this view, and the roots of hatred, jealousy, and envy will be cut off.

> Look upon your relatives with the same frame of mind, so your heart can burn now in mourning for their dying breaths. That which must happen will happen. So consider that it's already happened; act from the assumption that your friend is already breathing his last and is about to die.

> If there's anything holding you back from adopting this insight, then eject those feelings from your heart. If you find that you cannot expel them through your own efforts, don't just stand there doing nothing. Know that for every one who cannot do something, there is a great Enabler (and that is God).

> The inability to act is like a chain. He's the One Who laid it upon you. Therefore, you have to open your eyes to the One Who laid the chain upon you. Humbly beseech Him, saying, "O Giver of Guidance! I once was free, and now I've fallen into bondage. Why? I've planted my foot in the wrong place, and by Your Power, I'm slipping backward all the time. I've been deaf to Your warnings, even as I professed to be holy. In truth, I've been nothing but sacrilegious. Am I to look more on the things You've created or upon Death (which is the harbinger of what is real)? Death is like the autumn, and You are like the source of the leaves."

> For years, Death has been beating the drum; only when time is running out will you listen? In his anguish, the careless person will cry out from deep within, saying, "Oh my! I'm dying!" Has Death

only made you aware of that now? Death's throat is hoarse from all the shouting; his drum is cracked from the severe blows he's laid upon it. But you wrapped yourself up in trivial things. Only now will you realize the mystery of dying.

Mathnawi VI, 761–776

We Were Not Made for This World

This world is like a sauna that's become too hot, so much so that you feel uncomfortable and your soul starts to melt. Even though the sauna is wide and spacious, your soul is distressed and pummeled by the heat. You feel no sense of relief until you come out of it, so what does it matter how wide the room is for you?

It's the same as if you put on a tight pair of shoes, O mistaken one, and went for a walk in a wide desert. The vastness of the desert seems to narrow in on you so much so that it becomes like a prison for you.

Anyone who sees you from far away might think, "He's blossoming like a flower in that desert." Yet, he doesn't know that while you appear to be in a rose garden, just like the damned, your soul is in quiet lamentation. Your only way to rejuvenate is to take those shoes off, for only then will your soul be free of the body for a while.

Mathnawi III, 3545–3552

The Lure of Impossible Dreams

All the people in the world are running away from their freedom of choice and self-awareness into their blind (pleasure-driven) drunkenness.

In order to "save" themselves from having to see things clearly, they fill their lives with disgraceful behavior like drunks and carouse without end.

Everyone should know that this kind of life is a trap in which willfulness and the memory (of what they have done) is a living hell.

They're running away from facing themselves and they become selfish in the process with drunkenness or some other maniacal addiction. Take notice, O you moral soul!

Mathnawi VI, 224–227

Don't Fight Life—It's Not Your Battle

This world is like holding bits of straw in the hand; (the straw) is subject to the power of the wind, which is the unseen (force that moves it about).

(Similarly, the world) is a helpless object under the whim and power of the unseen. (He) makes (the world) sometimes high, sometimes low, sometimes whole, and sometimes broken. He pushes it to the right, then to the left, and sometimes brings out roses, and other times, thorns.

See how the hand is hidden, while the pen (of destiny) writes. See the horse galloping, while the rider remains out of sight. See the arrow as it soars, while the bow is nowhere to be found. See individual souls before you, while the Soul above all souls remains unseen.

Don't break the arrow, for it's the arrow of a King. It wasn't shot from afar for nothing, for it was loosed by the thumb of One Who knows (how to hit His mark). God told (Muhammad), "It wasn't you who threw," for God's actions take precedence over our own.

Break your anger, don't break the arrow. Your angry eye thinks milk is blood! Give the arrow a kiss and bring it to the King, wipe the bloodstained arrow, even as it still drips with your blood. What you can see is helpless, trapped, and weak, while what you cannot see is strong and without limits.

Mathnawi II, 1300–1309

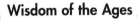

> ### Wisdom of the Ages
>
> Rumi wrote these lines in his *Divan*: "O my heart, why are you a captive of the earth that's passing away? Fly out of this cage, since you're a bird of the spiritual realm. You're my closest friend, hiding behind the secret veil. Why do you make your home in this temporary place? Look at what you really are; go out and travel from the prison of the physical world to the boundless meadow of ideas!"

Materialism Is a Plague Upon Our Souls

The pull of possessions is strong. We are, by nature, an acquisitive species. Our ancestors hoarded nuts and berries to stave off famine. If each of us took a look at everything we own right now, we might come away thinking that, as a species, we haven't evolved very much since then! Rumi warned against hoarding material goods in so many ways. For example, he wrote this:

> Whoever is awake to the material world is asleep to the spiritual world. His wakefulness is worse than his sleeping! When our souls are not awake to God, then our wakefulness to other things is like closing our doors (to guidance).
>
> *Mathnawi* I, 409–410

That's the crux of the problem. If someone gives you a hiking map to reach a distant destination, but then you decide to bring a heavy load with you on your hike, when it's time to start walking, what do you think will happen? You clear your understanding when you clear your hands of useless junk. As long as physical objects distract you from examining your soul, you'll never feel truly satisfied with life, no matter how many more distractions you fill it with. Now let us survey some of the insights Rumi had on this topic.

Dimming the Light of the Soul

A simple man heard the sound of footsteps in his house at night. He took up a flint to start a flame so he could see.

Just then, the thief came and sat down next to him, and whenever the tinder was about to catch fire, the thief put it out by pressing the tip of his finger on it so the spark would disappear.

The good man thought the fire was dying by itself, for he never saw the thief there putting it out. The man said, "This tinder must be wet, for on account of it the spark goes out at once."

Because it was dark all around him, he never saw the fire extinguisher sitting next to him. In the same way, the person who is (materialistic) doesn't see a similar fire extinguisher in his heart.

Mathnawi VI, 357–363

The Real Root of Stress

All the pain that occupies our hearts comes from the fog and dust of our existence, blown along by the winds (of our material desires). These unsettling sources of angst are like a reaper's blade to us; all our preoccupation with *this* and *that* is a constant source of temptation for us (to acquire more and more).

Know that every pain you feel is a part of Death, so drive that portion of Death from yourself, if at all possible! Whenever you cannot flee from a part of Death, know that the whole of it will be dumped upon your head! On the other hand, if a part of Death has been made sweet to you, then know that God will make all of it sweet to you.

Pain comes from Death like a messenger, (reminding you not to be so materialistic). Don't turn your face away from the messenger, you foolish one! Whoever lives in material splendor dies in bitterness. Whoever serves only the body loses his soul.

Mathnawi I, 2296–2302

The Cause of Human Conflict

God gave colors, variety, and value to the earth, and this causes the childish at heart to fight over it. When a piece of dough is baked into the shape of a camel or a lion, children bite their fingers in their greed for it. The lion or camel will turn to soggy bread in the mouth, but it's pointless to tell that to children.

Children are in perpetual ignorance, whimsy, and doubt—thank God that they're not that strong! Children are prone to argument and mischief—thank God they have little skill and ability!

Ah, but think of all those childish elders who lack discipline, who in their strength have become an affliction upon every guardian! When weapons and ignorance are brought together, the wielder of both becomes a tyrant who consumes the world like a pharaoh.

O poor person! Be thankful for your lack of means, for you've been saved from becoming an ungrateful pharaoh. Thank God that you're the oppressed and not the oppressor, for you're safe from acting like a pharaoh and safe from endless temptations.

An empty stomach never boasted of being a god, for it has no wood to feed the fire. An empty stomach is the Devil's prison, for the constant anxiety for bread keeps him from plotting and scheming.

Mathnawi VI, 4717–4727

Wisdom of the Ages

Rumi was a strong advocate of living the simple life. He once wrote in his *Divan* the following lines: "The fewer complications we lay upon our hearts and hands, the more we disengage from the world around us, the happier we'll find ourselves. A poor man's pleasure, though gone in an instant, is still better than all the pageantry of a thousand kings."

Learning to Fight Materialism

Once you've accepted that the material objects of this world are nothing more than a distraction from your real purpose in life, you then may ask how you can be relieved of an over-emphasis on materialism. Well, by recognizing the dangers of it, you've already won half the battle. Indeed, Rumi's teachings have already settled in your heart. You've already begun to understand what he expressed in the following words:

This world is like a tree, O gracious ones, and we're like half-ripened fruit upon it. Unripe fruits hold tightly to the branch, for in their immaturity they're not ready for the palace (table). After they've become sweet and fully ripened, then they bite their lips pensively and release their hold on the branch.

When a mouth has been sweetened by that kind of contentment, the kingdom of the world becomes less alluring to people. To hold on too tightly to the world is a sign of not being ripe yet. As long as you remain an embryo, your only job will be to suck blood.

Mathnawi III, 1293–1297

In a comical sort of way, Rumi also advised us to keep these words in mind:

The best plan for a prisoner is to dig a hole in his cell to escape. If he fills in the hole, then that would be a waste of his time. This world is a prison, and we're the prisoners. Dig a hole and escape!

Mathnawi I, 981–982

That's just it! The best thing a person can do in this life is to find a way for his or her soul to escape it intact and illuminated. There isn't much time to unlock the spirit, so it's time to stop filling in our only means of escape and instead get busy removing the baubles and trinkets from our lives. Now we will take a look at Rumi's advice on how to combat the pull of materialism. As you read these passages, think deeply on the meaning and imagine how you can make this wisdom a part of your life. Though progress may be slow and imperceptible at times, still the steady rise of awareness will not diminish within the one who has already seen a glimmer of the light within his or her soul.

Moderate Your Work

Don't work overly hard to accomplish worldly affairs; don't work so hard in any business that's not spiritual in nature.

If you (concentrate too much on the material world), then you'll leave this world incomplete, with your (spiritual) affairs lacking and your bread left unbaked besides!

The beautifying of your grave and tombstone isn't done through stone or wood or plaster. No, not at all! Rather, it's when you dig your grave in purity and bury your self-centeredness in His center.

When you become His dust, when you're buried in His love, then your breath can be replenished in His. A tomb with domes and towers—that's no good for people who know what the truth is!

Look at someone who wears soft silk: does that silk help him understand anything at all? His soul may be in abject torment, while the scorpion of grief stings his empty heart. On the outside, he's all fanciness and decoration; yet inside he's in utter misery from his tortured thoughts.

On the contrary, you might see someone else who is wearing old clothes, all patched up and worn, yet, his thoughts may be as sweet as sugarcane and his words like sugar!

Mathnawi III, 128–137

You Don't Have to Renounce the World!

To find a treasure is a rare thing and betrays the hand of luck. In truth, a person has to earn his livelihood for as long as the body is able.

How does having a job prevent anyone from discovering a treasure? Don't retire from work, for that hidden treasure may be following close behind.

Mathnawi II, 734–735

Beware of the Sweet Lure

On every side, there's a phantom calling out to you—"Listen, my friend! If you want direction, come over here! I'll show you the way. I'll be your companion. I'm your steady guide on this winding path."

But that phantom is not your guide, and it won't show you the way. You who are like Joseph (in the face of your jealous brothers), don't go to the wolves!

Good sense is in not letting yourself be fooled by the abundance, sweet things, and traps of the hotel, for she has neither bounty nor sweets. She chants her incantations and whispers in your ears, saying, "Come on in; be my guest. You're the light of my heart. My house is yours and you, well, you are mine!"

Good sense is when you say to her, "My stomach hurts," or "I'm not feeling well. This stale air is making me sick," or "My head hurts; help me get rid of my headache," or "My cousin is calling me to come over."

To be sure, she'll give you a taste of honey studded with poison stings; but in the end her honey will leave you full of sores. It doesn't matter if she gives you 50 or 60 gold coins, for in the end, O fish, she gives you nothing more than flesh on a hook.

Mathnawi III, 216–225

Avoid the Ultimate Regret

The Prophet said that no one who leaves this world feels sorrow or regret because of the act of dying, but because he's filled with regret from having missed the opportunity (to perfect his soul).

Such a one will say to himself, "Why didn't I pay attention to death, the real destination for every blessing and material good? Even though I was gifted with both inner and outer sight, why did I devote all my life's attention to those phantoms that disappeared at the fated hour?"

The regret of the dead is not because of the act of dying; it's because they realized: "We gave all our attention to material things."

Mathnawi VI, 1450–1454

Rumi's References

Rumi often used the metaphor that this life is like a dream in comparison to the reality that an awakened mind will see. The source for this allusion is a tradition of Muhammad in which he said, "People are asleep in this world; when they die, they will wake up."

The Real Treasure That Lasts

Standards of beauty and success in this world hold no permanence in the great scheme of things. Haven't we all heard the message that those things are fleeting and cannot last? Yet, so many are drawn to those things and focus on them as if they were forever. This is the pull of our animal nature that focuses only on the form. Rumi poignantly described where true beauty and success lie in these words:

> Radiance and glory is found within the beautiful faces of the sincere; their bodies may pass away, yet their beauty remains until the Day of Judgment.

> The only one who is truly ugly is the one who remains ugly forever. The only one who is truly beautiful is the one who remains beautiful forever. The beautiful one is always laughing; the ugly one is always frowning.

> *Mathnawi* VI, 4715–4716

Reap the Best Rewards

Now let us conclude this discussion with some parting nuggets of wisdom from the Master. Pay close attention to how he emphasizes the true rewards that a life well lived can offer.

> This world is like a playground, and death is the onset of night; you come home exhausted at the end of the day with an empty purse. The earnings of spirituality are love, inner joy, and the ability to accept the Light of God, you stubborn one!

> Your lowly materialistic soul wants you to earn what will pass away. How long will you earn what is so low? Let it go! Enough already!

Beware, if your lowly materialistic soul ever prompts you to earn something noble, then there must be some kind of trick or scheme behind it.

Mathnawi II, 2600–2603

Let Your Heart Carry You Forward

There once was a hermit who lived in the mountains. Solitude was his bedfellow and his closest friend. Because tranquility was coming to him from the Creator, he grew tired of the company of others.

Just as staying home is easy for some, so, too, is traveling easy for others. In the same way that you're in love with power and control, another person finds pleasure in simple occupations.

Everyone's been made for a particular kind of work, and the desire for that work has been implanted within his heart. How can the hand and foot be set in motion without this desire? How can branches or bits of straw be moved without wind or rain?

If you find that your desire is propelling you toward heaven, then unfold the wings of your majesty, like a great mythical bird. If, however, you find that your desire never rises above the earth, then wallow in sadness, and never cease to cry.

The wise are the ones who cry in the beginning; the foolish beat their ends in the end. From the outset of any endeavor, see where it will all end, so that on the Day of Judgment you won't find yourself in sorrowful regret.

Mathnawi III, 1615–1623

The Least You Need to Know

◆ Materialism is a blinder on our understanding of the self. As long as it remains, we will be blind to our inner potential as spiritual beings.

◆ Materialism and greed are the main sources for conflict both within a person's own heart and on a wider scale in human society.

◆ Life is short. Only when a person ruminates upon this and fully accepts it can she begin to free herself from the shackles of materialism.

◆ It's not required to renounce the world to be more spiritual. All that's required is a shift in emphasis: less focus on things, and more focus on polishing the self.

Part 3

Love and the Single Mind

Human beings are creatures with a need to love and be loved.
Yet how often does love elude us, even as we sometimes forget
how to love? Sometimes the answer to this dilemma is simply
asking, "Then what is love?" We often mistake other things for
it, and we don't always recognize it when it comes our way. Rumi
was keenly aware of this problem.

According to Rumi, love begins from the awakened mind. When
the mind is open, it guides the heart and teaches it how to listen
to the fleeting Divine echo that lies just at the edges of sight.
Once the hand that was lost in darkness begins to touch the
subtlety of pure love, a torrent of desire for it erupts. Don't try
to regulate it; don't try to understand. In this part Rumi teaches
you how to master it and bring joy to your life for the rest of
your days.

Chapter 7

Understanding the Nature of Love and Pain

In This Chapter

◆ What Rumi had to say about Divine love and its application to daily life

◆ How to recognize the signs of love in one's self and others, and how love is expressed in various circumstances

◆ The many different ways in which God's love is present in our lives, including the hidden blessings and lessons of hardship

◆ How the principles of unconditional love can guide you in your interactions with others

Love is the basic foundation of the natural world. This is a theme passionately laid out in Rumi's many writings, and it underlies the basis of his philosophy. From the smallest to the largest creature in the web of life, love, in some form or another, is the essential energy that binds each of them to their fellows, and enables them to survive. Also, where there is pain, it could be the result of love, for the lion takes the gazelle not in hate, but in love of its own offspring. Only human beings, of all creatures, can infuse their actions with love or disparage them with hate.

In Rumi's worldview, because we human beings were given a soul on loan from God and a conscious will to understand the concepts of justice and injustice, we have a special responsibility to polish and purify ourselves from the worst in our primal or animalistic nature. One of the ways to elevate our spirit and embrace the concepts of essential goodness and justice is to increase our understanding of what ethereal love is and how to make it grow. In this chapter, we will explore Rumi's thoughts on how to accomplish these and other similar goals. As you read through the selections, consider how the lessons could apply to your own life, for in becoming more expansive within the heart and learning to recognize pain for the teacher that it is, we not only uplift those around us, we uplift ourselves, as well.

Recognizing Love for What It Is

Love on the philosophical level has many facets. Love is both a state of being and an internal disposition. In our modern world, the concept of love has been cheapened to a degree as to render it almost meaningless. Love is more than mere affection, physical attraction, or focused longing. Love is the consummate willingness to forgo one's own desires and goals for the welfare and benefit of another. It's the belief in the ultimate good that can be found in all people, no matter how far they seem to have fallen. It's the attitude that no matter the consequences or outcomes, there is nothing material in this world that's worth sullying one's soul or character for. In short, love is the foundation of integrity and the cornerstone of our basic sense of justice and goodness in this world.

Wisdom of the Ages

Rumi wrote of the phenomenon of pure, platonic friendships in these words: "When words come easily from the heart, that's a sign of true friendship. When words are hard to find, that's the sign of distance. A heart that's been exposed to affection, how can it remain bitter? When a nightingale comes upon a rose, how can it remain silent?"
—*Mathnawi* VI, 2638–2639

A purified soul is capable of making connections with other creatures that transcend mere physical attraction or casual friendship. In the classical sense, it provides a way for people to read each other's souls on a deeper level. Rumi wrote much on this issue, and in various ways he showed some of the characteristics of this type of soul and how it behaved. Let us now take a walk through the various ways and means Rumi identified that can help us to acquire a truly loving nature. For Rumi, this inner transformation is one of the prime requirements for becoming a wise and noble soul.

Let the Heart Open to the Light

When I pray I retreat to a solitary place and ask the Knower of all mysteries about my affairs. It's my frequent routine to turn (to God) like this in prayer, and thus I experience the true meaning of the phrase, "Delight is felt in prayer."

The window of my soul is opened, and from the pristine (beauty of true faith), the meaning of God's scripture pours over me without any intermediary. The scripture, the healing rain, and the Light (of God) fall through my window into my house from within myself.

The house that has no windows is a hell. Make a window, O you servant (of truth), for that's the foundation of the (spiritual) way of life. Don't swing your axe at every tangled bush; come now, swing your axe and carve out a window.

Mathnawi III, 2401–2405

Intentions Mean More Than Appearances

Even if you fumble in your words of praise, God still accepts the efforts of those who have little to give. God will accept even a crust of bread and forgive the one who offered it. Isn't it true that from the eyes of the blind, two drops of light are enough?

Mathnawi III, 2115–2116

The Importance of a Thankful Nature

Giving thanks for what you have is better than what you received in the first place. How can a thankful person be focused solely on the material goods he receives?

Thankfulness is at the heart of material blessings, for material blessings are just the shell. Thankfulness is what brings you closer to the realm of the Beloved. Too much success produces heedlessness, while thankfulness produces alertness. Seek your fortune with the net of gratitude to the King.

Mathnawi III, 2895–2897

Learn Love from the Experts

Fix within your spirit love for righteous souls; don't give your heart to anyone save for those whose hearts are filled with joy.

Don't go to the neighborhood of despair, for there is always hope. Don't go toward the darkness, for there are always more suns (to shine upon you).

The heart will lead you into the neighborhood of spiritual people, while the body will lead you toward the prison of water and dirt.

Truly, you should feed your heart with the words of those who are in agreement with its needs. Go now; look for those who are spiritually advanced, so they may help you become the same.

Mathnawi I, 723–726

This Love Can Be Bought

The motive for doing any kind of business rests upon hope and chance, even though they may wear their necks thin from the constant work.

When a businessperson goes to his place of work in the morning, he runs there quickly in the hope and chance of earning his livelihood.

If there wasn't at least the chance of earning your livelihood, why would you even go there? Of course, there's always the danger of disappointment, so how strong you have to be!

In this quest for your daily bread, has the fear of disappointment made you too weak to conduct your search?

"Oh, no!" you say. "For even though I'm afraid of disappointment, the fear is even harder on me when I'm doing nothing. When I'm at work, at least my hope for success is greater. When I'm doing nothing, the risk of failure is that much more."

So now, O deprived one, why is the fear of disappointment holding you back from engaging in the search for the spirit?

Haven't you seen the tremendous gains made by the people in our market, such as the gains made by the prophets and the saints?

What outstanding opportunities have come to them by going to this kind of store, and how great are the profits they've made in this business!

Mathnawi III, 3093–3101

> **Rumi's References**
>
> Rumi often couched his teachings in references to economic matters, especially trading. His boyhood home was located on the fabled Silk Road, so he grew up with merchants, caravans, and trade goods all around him from an early age.

To What End Your Life's Work?

What do you own and what have you gained? What pearls have you snatched from the bottom of the sea?

On the day of your death all your senses will vanish; will you have any spiritual light that will be your heart's companion?

When dirt fills your eyes in the grave, will you have what you need to make your grave illuminated?

When your hands and feet rot away to nothing, will you have the wings and feathers for your soul to fly on high?

The lower animal soul will pass away; it's your duty to have pre-
pared an everlasting spirit to take its place.

The verse that says, "The one who does good will be rewarded 10
times as much," is not dependent only upon doing good, but upon
bringing that good into God's presence.

You possess both a human and an animal nature, so which one will
you nurture? How can you only bring your accidental actions that
have merely passed away?

Mathnawi II, 939–945

Why Does Love Sometimes Involve Pain?

Despair and stress come from the heart. But what is the source of
that inner pain which arises solely from within? When we feel empty,
unfulfilled, or realize the meaning of something and how it may
affect us or those we love, then pain and stress can arise. Pain is our
reminder, however, that we have something to change, either within
ourselves, or in the world around us. To ignore the message of pain is
to invite nothing but more of the same. Rumi advised this:

Pain comes from examining ourselves from within; pain brings us
out of the veil of self-conceit. Unless a mother is overwhelmed in
pain, how can the child be born? This trust is in the heart, and the
heart is full of advice just like a midwife. The midwife may say that
the woman has no pain, but pain is a prerequisite, for pain makes a
way for the child to be born. The one who has no pain is a villain,
for to be without pain is to say, "I am God."

Mathnawi II, 2517–2521

Thus, pain is a teacher. In every aspect of life, if something causes
us pain, we must address the root of it. Until we do, our heart will
be unsettled and our peace of mind will be disturbed. When the
hand touches a hot pan on the stove, would you expect the person
to ignore the pain? Of course not! You would think, and hope, she
would take action immediately to remove what's hurting her. So what's
your excuse? Isn't life too short to spend one moment of it in mental

anguish? Pain is providing a wake-up call to take action. Thus, even pain is an expression of love, for it makes you see things more clearly and motivates you to rise up and improve your situation.

Rumi's References

There are several important sayings of Muhammad that Sufis use as the basis for explaining the existence of pain, sorrow, and hardship in the world. Among these is this one: "When God loves somebody, He tests him with trials and hardships." The reward for perseverance in the face of setbacks is Paradise.

Don't Let Pain Overcome Your Hope in God

Whatever strikes come down upon you from Heaven, live in the expectation that you'll receive some kind of a noble gift afterward. He is not the kind of King who will strike you and then not give you a crown or a throne upon which you may recline.

This world isn't worth as much as a gnat's wing; yet, an eternal reward is granted for the sake (of enduring) each strike suffered here. Wriggle your neck out of this golden collar of life and take all your lumps that come from God.

The prophets suffered many a strike on the back of their necks; yet, on account of their hardships, they were able to hold their heads up high.

As you weather the challenges of life, then be cognizant within yourself (of the purpose of setbacks), O young one, so that God can find you at home (when He's ready to reward you). If you don't, then He'll leave, taking His noble gifts with Him, saying, "I didn't find anyone in the house."

Mathnawi VI, 1638–1644

Pain Spurs Us to Action

The servant complains to God of pain and affliction; in 100 ways, he groans.

Yet God says to him, "What's this? Your sorrow and pain have brought you to humbly supplicate before Me, and they've made you righteous. Rather, you should complain of all the good fortune that comes your way, steering you as it does, far away from My door until ultimately you've been made an outcast from My presence."

The truth is that every enemy of yours is a kind of remedy for you; he's a cure and a benefit who has your best interests at heart. Yet, you flee from him to some silent place and beseech God to show you mercy. It's your friends who may really be your enemies, for they take you away from God's presence by keeping you occupied with them.

> **Wisdom of the Ages**
>
> Rumi wrote: "God created pain and sadness so that joy could be clearly recognized on account of what's opposite to it. Hidden things are thus made apparent through the agency of their opposites; but since God has no opposite, only He remains obscure."
> —*Mathnawi* I, 1130–1131

There is an animal called a porcupine; it grows stronger and expands in size when it's hit with a stick. The more you strike at it, the more it seems to thrive. It grows larger and larger from the hits of a stick.

In the same way, the soul of a faithful believer is like a porcupine, for it's made stronger and more expansive after experiencing the strikes of (life's) hardships.

Mathnawi IV, 91–99

Help Is Available

Pain has a cure, even if we don't see the remedy at the moment. The world is full of remedies, but you'll find no cure unless God opens a window for you.

Even though you may be ignorant of the medicine right now, God will reveal it in your time of need. Didn't the Prophet say that for every ailment, God has created a cure?

Mathnawi II, 682–684

Remembrance Is an Elixir

If you ever feel frozen within, remember God. Remembering God brings thoughts to life, so make remembrance the sunlight that will melt your petrified emotions.

Even though the tug of God is the original source for your awakening, yet still push yourself onward to action, my fellow servant. Don't rely only upon that tug, for if you give up taking an active role in your affairs, it will be as a snub (to God). How can snubbing God be proper for one of His devoted lovers?

O young one, give no thought to acceptance or denial; rather keep focused on God's will and His prohibitions. Carry on in this fashion until suddenly, the bird of (Divine) attraction darts from her nest and comes your way. Put out the candle the moment you see the sunrise.

When the eyes become beams of light, it's the light (of God's wisdom upon you); from within the husk it sees even the kernels. In a speck, it sees the whole sun; in a drop it holds the whole ocean.

Mathnawi VI, 1475–1482

Be Merciful to Those in Pain

If you desire tears, then be merciful to the one who is weeping. If you desire mercy, then be merciful to the weak.

Mathnawi I, 822

Do Not Be a Cause for Injustice

Whenever you feel pain, ask for God's forgiveness. By the command of the Creator, pain is a powerful motivator.

Whenever God wills, pain can become a source of joy; slavery becomes a kind of freedom.

Air, earth, water, and fire are slaves of God. To you and me they're dead, but to God they're alive.

In God's sight, fire is always at the ready; writhing ceaselessly by day and by night, like someone devoted to love.

If you strike stone and iron together, sparks of fire leap out. It's by the command of God that fire jumps out like that.

Don't strike the stone and iron of injustice together, for these two produce men and women who are likewise unjust.

Stone and iron are sources of fire, but you should look even higher, O my good soul.

Mathnawi I, 836–842

Reform the Self Above All Others

O you who treat others badly simply because of your high status; know that you're digging a hole for yourself to fall into. Don't weave a cocoon (of false pretenses) around yourself like a silk-worm; you're digging a hole for yourself! Don't dig so eagerly!

Many of the evils that you see in others are really just a reflection of your own evil in them. In their reflection, all your hypocrisy, evil, and arrogance are made apparent. You're the real wicked one! You're aiming blows at yourself and laying curses upon your own head at every turn.

You don't recognize the evil within yourself at all, for if you did you would hate yourself to the very core. You're assaulting your-self, you fool, like a deceived lion who rushed at himself upon see-ing his reflection in a pool.

O you who see bad reflections in the face of your uncle, your uncle is not the bad one, it's you, so don't run away from facing your own self.

The Prophet said that the faithful are mirrors of each other. If you hold a blue colored glass before your eyes, then the world appears blue to you. Unless you're blind, you must recognize that this blueness comes from within your own self. Speak of the evil within yourself before you ever speak of the evil in others.

Mathnawi I, 1311–1312, 1319–1324, 1327–1330

Wisdom of the Ages

Rumi was a strong proponent of prayer. He once wrote: "Stand and pray at night, for you are like a candle, and at night a candle stands and burns." He also engaged in frequent prayer himself, often spending hours in quiet devotion.

Don't Misrepresent Yourself

There are hundreds of thousands of trials, O child, for the one who says, "I'm in charge of the gate." Even if fools don't test him, then experts will always ask him for proof.

When an unskilled person pretends to be a tailor, the king will throw down a piece of silk before him, saying, "Sew this into a wide vest." Because of this test (which he cannot pass), he is put to shame.

Mathnawi III, 682–684

Seek the Silver Lining

If you're not well known in this world, it doesn't mean that you're lost; God knows His servants best. A golden treasure is kept safe when it's hidden in a lonely, forgotten place. Who would place a treasure out in the open? Likewise, it is often said, "Happiness is hidden under sorrow."

Mathnawi III, 1132–1134

No One Can Help You but You

There is a basket of bread upon your head, yet you're begging for crusts from every door. Look to your own head, and leave off childish ways. Go and knock on the door of your own heart. Why are you knocking on everyone else's door?

Mathnawi V, 1073–1074

The Soothing Mercy of God

At first, the devil was my teacher, and soon he was no more than a puff of air compared to me.

God saw all of this sinfulness of mine, but then He transformed it as if He never saw it so He could avoid embarrassing me.

Mercy repaired the shredded cloak of my piety, and draped me in repentance sweeter than life itself.

Whatever sins I had committed before, mercy considered them as never having occurred. Whatever duties I had failed to do, mercy considered them done.

Mercy made me as free and pure as the cypress and the lily; it filled my heart with a sense of fortune and joy.

It wrote my name in the Book of the Righteous. I had been destined for Hell; yet it gave me Paradise.

When I had cried, "I've fallen to the very bottom of the pit," my cry became a rope, and that rope was lowered down into my dark hole.

I took hold of that rope and climbed out. I became happy and strong, committed and cheerful.

Once I was lying in misery at the bottom of a pit; now I've transcended the whole world! Praise be to You, O God, for you carried me far from my distress.

Even if the tip of every hair of mine could gain the power to speak, that still wouldn't express the amount of thanks due to You.

Among the gardens and fountains of Paradise, I'm crying out to all humanity, "Oh, if only my people knew about all of this!"

Mathnawi V, 2305–2316

Unraveling Divine Mysteries

Part of Rumi's joyous ecstasy of faith was in his fascination with the many twists and turns and odd quirks of Divine expression to be found in life. A poor man stumbles upon a diamond in the road. A strong man becomes frail in the midst of celebrating his power. Love opens up in the most unexpected places. These are the kinds of things that Rumi commented upon in many passages of his books. Here is a selection of some of his more memorable observations.

The Mystery of Misplaced Expectations

O you who have your hopes firmly set on one source of income, saying, "My fruit will come to me from that high tree over there." Your hope won't be realized from there; no, not at all, for your provision may come from another place entirely.

So why did God plant this seed of hope within you, if He doesn't provide for you from where you had planned? It's for a clever reason and purpose, and also so that your heart may be constantly perplexed.

Indeed, O you who would learn, it's so your heart will be perplexed by its uncertainty as to the source from where its desires will next be fulfilled, and also so that you can realize the extent of your weakness and ignorance. This causes your faith in the Hidden Realm to increase.

In addition, it's like this so that your heart can be perplexed over the source and timing of its expected benefits, as well as so it can be curious about what (God) will produce from this hope.

You hope to earn your living through tailoring, and plan to earn money for the rest of your life in this way; yet, He makes your daily bread come to you from the jewelry business—something you never would have imagined!

So how was it that your hopes had been set on tailoring, while He never intended that your daily bread should come to you from that source?

It was through some amazing plan contrived in the knowledge of God—an order that He recorded in the recesses of time, so that your thoughts should be ever perplexed, and so your confusion should ever be present in your mind.

Mathnawi VI, 4190–4201

Footprints of the Master

The night that Rumi passed away (December 17, 1273) was nick-named by his followers, *Sebul Arus*, which means the *Night of Union*. Mevlevi Sufis have commemorated this day with great fanfare ever since.

Opposites Serve a Purpose

God keeps turning you from one emotion to another, revealing the existence of each through the process of alternation. This is so that fear of the left side can bring forth the joy of the verse, "He causes them to hope for salvation from the right side." He does this so you can have two wings, for a bird with only one wing cannot fly.

Mathnawi II, 1552–1554

What Love Sometimes Brings

I often wonder at the seeker of purity, who shies away from harsh treatment when it's time to be polished. Love is like a lawsuit; rough handling is the evidence of its passing. Where there is no evidence, the case is lost.

Don't feel wronged when this Judge demands your evidence. In order to unlock this treasure, you sometimes have to kiss a snake. The rough handling is not directed toward you personally, O child; no, not at all, but rather it's directed toward the bad quali-ties you harbor within. When a man beats a rug, his strikes are not directed at the rug, but at all the dust it contains.

Mathnawi III, 4008–4012

There's No Stopping Love

The caravan of love moves forward when travelers join in on the jour-ney. Through the triumphs and tribulations of life, a stronger love emerges. Rumi believed in the redemptive power of unconditional love. When love becomes so deep that you cannot even bear the thought to harm an insect for no reason or tear a leaf for no purpose, then you have approached the threshold of the kind of love Rumi was talking about. In the following selections, let's join him in his celebration of pure and unadulterated love.

You Are More Than You See

If you look only at the form, you see the image of a man. Look at all the bewildered people of Greece or Khorasan. "Turn toward your Lord," He said. Turning means peering within, and to see more than just a mere man.

From the *Divan*

👣 Footprints of the Master

In Rumi's house there was a great central pillar. When he was feeling a sense of spiritual ecstasy coming over him, he would sometimes take hold of that pillar and slowly spin around it while composing verses for the *Mathnawi*. Because of this, Mevlevi Sufis sometimes place a ceremonial post as a prop for their rituals.

Don't Go Empty-Handed

The currency that this world requires in the market is gold. The currency of the next life is love and two eyes wet from tears. Whoever arrives in the market of the next life without any currency will lose his life and quickly come away disappointed.

Mathnawi VI, 839–840

Burn Down the House of the Ego

How can this heart be happy until I burn (away all of its selfishness to make room for God)? My heart is His home and place of residence.

If you would burn your own house down, then burn it! Who can say, "That's not right!"

Burn the house of (your ego) to ashes, O raging lion. A lover's house will be made the better for it.

From now on, I'm going to make this burning (of my selfish desires) my sole aim, for I'm like a candle now, and I'm made brighter from burning.

Mathnawi VI, 617–623

Desire for Salvation Will Carry You There

Keep your hope directed toward the next life, dancing like a willow in your desire for Heaven. Both water and fire will rain down upon you from Heaven so your share of reward will go on increasing.

If your desire alone brings you there, it's really not so amazing. Don't be preoccupied with your weakness and look only to your ardent desire.

This quest is the trust of God that's been instilled within you, for everyone who seeks deserves to find what he's looking for.

Exert yourself so this desire to search will increase within you. Through this, your soul may escape from the prison of this body.

Mathnawi V, 1731–1735

The Least You Need to Know

◆ Love is the expression of the Divine will of God throughout all aspects of the universe. Only human beings can choose to open themselves to love or bury it within their soul.

◆ Part of learning to become a more loving person involves looking inward and turning the critical eye of self-examination upon one's own shortcomings.

◆ Hardship and pain are not as bad as they seem in themselves, for those are the things that give us the opportunity to grow.

◆ With no time to lose in this short life, the one who opens his or her heart to faith and awareness should not hesitate in letting the fruits of that inner awakening go to waste.

Chapter 8

Dancing with the Beloved

In This Chapter

◆ How Rumi expressed his joy and jubilation at his exuberant faith in God and in the goodness of the human soul

◆ Rumi's view of union with the divine in daily life and its meaning in success and hardship

◆ The nature of the joyful heart and the insights into life and love it can make

◆ How the enlightened soul does not fear death

The life awakened is a life that is fulfilling, rewarding, and imbued with meaning. Such is the benefit of unlocking the inner mysteries of the soul. Of course, it takes time to fully realize the fruits of more passionate and deliberate living, but when the harvest begins to bear fruit, the joy of its gardener is multiplied manifold. This was the crux of Rumi's teachings. Indeed, toward his later years of spiritual mastery, Rumi was filled with such light, such exuberance and understanding that those around him could literally see it in his face and sense it in his presence.

Rumi's followers, for example, could scarcely stand to be parted from him when he was engaged in other business.

While dictating the *Mathnawi*, his crowning achievement, Rumi would sometimes speak while spinning slowly and rhythmically in a circle. Other times he would narrate his poems while walking in the countryside or sitting in a quiet place. In all locations, Rumi was equally at peace. This is the special gift of the soul when it's been fully brought to life. This is the joy of union of which Rumi spoke. This chapter will showcase some of the most beautiful poems and insights that Rumi penned during his most insightful years of life. As you read through them, try to imagine a soul like Rumi's, rotating slowly, with arms raised in ecstasy, speaking words of inspired love. Then try to imagine your own soul doing the same. Perhaps you might catch a glimpse of the Master in your own rotations!

Celebrating Divine Love

How does one describe the beauty of the soul and its relationship to our conscious mind and character? Rumi examined this issue from many different perspectives and produced some very delightful passages in both the *Divan* and *Mathnawi* about it. The soul that opens itself to God soon realizes there is nothing else besides God. Such an enlightened soul then seeks to find its salvation in God, for that is where its true destination lies. Read on and revel in the delight that Rumi's words have to offer.

The Soul Knows How to Win

The rational mind says I'll win him with my logic.

Love says I'll win him with my silence.

The Soul says how can I ever hope to win him when I'm already his?

He wants for nothing; he worries not. He's not in search of a transcendent feeling of ecstasy. How can I win his heart with mere sweet wine or riches? He's not bound by what he feels, so how can I win him even with all the wealth of China?

He's an angel, though he looks like a man—even angels can't fly when he's around. How can I win him by imitating heavenly shapes?

He's held aloft on the wings of God; his food is radiant light. How can I win him with just a loaf of bread?

Neither a merchant is he, nor yet a craftsman, so how can I win him with fanciful designs or promises of high returns? He's not blind, nor readily duped, so how can I win him by faking illness in a bed?

Perhaps I'll go crazy, tear out my hair or mash my face in the dirt—but how could even these acts win him over? He sees everything around him, so how could I ever fool him so?

He looks not for fame, nor is he a king addicted to the applause of poets. How can I win him with mere skillful rhymes or poetic verse?

The radiance of his invisible form permeates the universe, so how can I win him with the meager promise of paradise?

Though I may fill the earth with rose petals, the ocean with tears, and assault the skies with thunderous praise of him, yet, none of these things will ever win him over.

The only way I can ever hope to win the heart of my beloved then—*is to give myself up to him.*

From the *Divan*

Wisdom of the Ages

While he was mourning the loss of Shamsuddin, Rumi wrote in his *Divan* these words: "Grant that I may become one with a true friend. Grant me the intelligence to stay away from love. Grant me the strength to challenge my own fate. Grant me the feet to walk away from this confused state."

Only Love Can Save You

O child, break your chains and be free! How long will you be a slave to silver and gold?

If you pour the ocean into a pitcher, how much of it can it hold? Only one day's supply at most. The pitcher, moved by the eye of greed, is never fully satisfied.

An oyster shell doesn't fill with pearls until it's learned to be content. Only the one who's had his shirt torn by Love is completely cured of greed and all imperfections.

We salute you, O Love, for you bring benefit to us all. You're the physician for all our ills—the cure for arrogance and pride. You're our Plato and our Galen at the same time!

Through Love, the physical body soars towards the heavens and the mountains become nimble and start to dance. Love inspired Mount Sinai, O lover, so much so that it became drunk and caused Moses to faint.

If I were ever joined by the lip to someone who felt as I do, I too, like the reed flute, would tell all that needs be told.

Whoever is far from me speaks in his own language and is stricken dumb with silence, even though he may know a hundred songs. When the rose is gone and the garden wilted away, you'll hear the tale of the nightingale no longer.

The Beloved is everything, and the one who loves Him is but a veil; the Beloved is alive, while the lover is dead. When Love no longer cares for him, he's left as a bird without wings. Oh, how unfortunate for him!

How can I know anything without the light of my Beloved in front of me and behind me? Yet, it's Love's plan that this message (of hope) goes forth.

If a mirror doesn't reflect the light that shines upon it, what could be the reason for that? Do you know why the mirror of your soul is not reflecting the light of Love? It's because you haven't cleared the rust away from its face!

Mathnawi I, 19–34

Beautify the Heart Through God

Listen, open a window to God, and bring joy to yourself by gazing upon Him through the opening.

It's love's task to make that window (in the heart), for the heart is illuminated by the beauty of the Beloved.

Mathnawi VI, 3095–3096

Do Something Extraordinary

You learned a skill to earn a living for the body, now learn a skill that will benefit the spirit, as well.

In this world you've clothed yourself in so many ways and become rich; when you leave this life, how will you fare then?

Learn a skill that will earn you God's forgiveness as your capital gain.

Mathnawi II, 2592–2594

Love Is Worth the Gamble

Love is unruly, though logic is not.

Logic always tries to make a profit.

Love is wild from the start and burns itself out without hesitation. When in trouble, love moves forward like a great millstone, firm and purposeful.

It snuffs out all sense of self-interest. It gambles everything away, never seeking any reward, even as it gains purity in exchange from Him.

God gives love its existence without cause, even as it gives the same back without cause.

Therefore, the sign of true devotion is to give without cause. This kind of gamble transcends the teachings of every religion.

Mathnawi VI, 1967–1974

Wisdom of the Ages _____

Rabi'ah al-Adawiyya (d. 801), an early female Muslim mystic, once said, "O Lord! If I worship You because I'm afraid of Hell, cast me into it. If I worship You because I desire Paradise, keep me from it. But if I worship you for Your own sake, then don't withhold from Me Your eternal Beauty."

We Belong to You

Our eyes overflow with tears at our separation from You; our souls are flooded with endless sighs.

An infant isn't fighting against its nurse when it cries; rather, it weeps without knowing either right or wrong.

We're like a harp that's played, strummed with a pick. Our lament originates from You, it doesn't come from within us.

We're like a flute, and the music we emit is from You. We're like a mountain, and our echo emanates from You.

We're like pieces on a chessboard charging to victory and defeat, yet, our winning and losing is due to You, O You most beautiful One!

Who are we, O Soul above all souls, that we should exist alongside of You? What are we—our very existence is really nothing at all. You're the eternal One who makes the temporary appear manifest.

We're like lions, though only lions on a banner, whose rippling in the wind gives the illusion of rushing onward every moment.

Their onward march can be seen, yet the wind that moves them remains unseen. May that unseen wind never fail!

Mathnawi I, 596–604

Swimming with the Current

According to Rumi's beliefs, God is omnipresent and aware of each individual creature in this vast universe. Consequently, God is concerned with the welfare of all those beings He created. Though He allows alternating bouts of hardship and success, ultimately, His purpose is to use such days of alternating fortune to provide opportunities for personal growth and improvement. The soul that is tested is the soul that finds a reason to move ahead in its understanding and ability.

Life is not random. In Rumi's worldview there is a rhythm and a reason to things. This means that any pain and loss that comes to us happens for a reason. Why shouldn't we be tested in this rough and tumble world? Who are we that we feel entitled to more than nature provides? In a physical existence, there will be physical challenges. The dormant soul only sees its immediate surroundings. It despairs when the frightening specter of imminent disaster is all it notices. The awakened soul looks ahead to the horizon, considering each success and setback as part of a long journey that will eventually reach somewhere. The key, then, is to realize that there is a force watching from an even higher perspective than that, and that one of the obstacles to a feeling of inner balance is the failure to recognize that presence.

For Rumi, when day-to-day affairs are placed within the context of a larger, universal trend or plan, then immediate concerns take on a less urgent tone. We are actors in our own right, but God sets the stage. Listen to Rumi's advice on how to learn to let go of the fear that comes from failing to see the end result of all accumulated experiences.

Look Ahead, O Traveler

The blind man takes each step in fear of tripping on a pothole; he walks on the road with a thousand fears. The one who can see has already seen how wide the road is, so he already knows about every rut and pothole. His legs and knees never shake, so how can he be disappointed by any hardship?

Mathnawi III, 1739–1741

Safety Is Found with God

He thought he was enough to handle it, but even though he was as strong as a mountain, a small flood swept him away.

When the command of destiny pokes its head out of heaven, even the most learned become blind and deaf; fish are thrown out of the sea; traps cruelly catch the bird as he flies; genies and devils are put back in their bottles; even the ruler of Babylon falls.

> **Rumi's References**
>
> Rumi was very familiar with the *Arabian Nights* tales. His allusion to genies in bottles is a reference to the story of *Aladdin and the Magic Lamp.*

Everyone is then lost, save for the one who's found safety within the command of destiny; no ill-reading of the planets ever touches him. Unless you find your safety within the command of destiny, then nothing you ever do can release you from it.

Mathnawi III, 468–473

At the Heart of the Matter

What is good sense? To be suspicious of the world. Whoever has good sense always expects disaster to strike, just like when a lion pops out of nowhere and seizes a man, dragging him back in the bush.

In that very instance, what will that man be thinking of? Consider this question well and be of like mind, O you who claim to know your religion. This lion, Destiny, is dragging our souls into the jungle, even as we're preoccupied with business and trade.

It seems that people are always afraid of getting poor, stuck as they are up to their throats in salt water! If they only paid attention to the One Who creates poverty, then the treasures of the earth would be opened for them.

Being afraid of hardship is in fact a kind of hardship in itself. In their quest for success in this material world, they've made themselves into nothing.

Mathnawi III, 2201–2207

Don't Deny the Keepers of Fate

In this world of searching and seeking, every type of person has been tied in the stable that suits him. If it strikes someone's fancy to bolt from his stable and invade the stable of others, right away the keen stableman seizes the edge of his leash and drags him back.

O sneaky one! If you haven't noticed your keepers, then look at the choices you have, and realize that they're not your own. You make choices, and your hands and feet seem free to act; but then you're held back, why?

You've taken to denying the keeper, and instead have labeled his (power over you) as, "Merely a lack of willpower."

Mathnawi III, 2077–2083

Mercy Never Gives Up

When the cleansing water has finished its battle, and it's become dirty so much so that no one wants to touch it, then God brings it back into the Ocean of Purity, so that the Water (of His love) can make it pure once more.

A year later it comes flowing back, (and when it's asked,) "Hey, where have you been?" It responds, saying, "In the Ocean of Purity! I left here dirty, and I've come back clean. I've been wrapped in the cloak of honor, and I return to earth once more."

"Listen!" (the Water says.) "Come to me all you who are tainted, for my soul has been exposed to the nature of God. I'll accept all your foul nature and transform the demon within you into a pure angel.

"Whenever I become sullied, I return back (to Him) once more—to the original Source of all purities. Once there, I'll tear this filthy robe off my head, and He'll give me one as pure as snow once more."

This is the work (of God), and my task is the same—He is the Lord of all Creation, and the beautifier of the world!

Mathnawi V, 199–207

Realize the Self Is Nothing

You sweeten your taste buds with the flavor of false imagination. You blow into the bag of ego and inflate it. Then suddenly, with the prick of a needle, your windbag is deflated—let no smart person ever have a body as big as this!

Mathnawi III, 719–720

All Beings Depend upon God

O (God), the One Who makes demands within my heart, like an embryo (makes demands within the womb)—since You're making demands of me, make my task easy!

For me to fulfill this task, show me the way, give me guidance, or else cancel these demands and lay no more burdens upon me! Since You're demanding gold from a pauper, at least give him some gold in secret, O King!

Without You, how can poetry and rhyme ever come forth at night or at dawn? Poetry, harmony, and rhymes, O Knower of All, are mere timid slaves at Your command, in that You've made all things to glorify You, whether they're conscious or not.

Everything glorifies You in a different way, and one thing doesn't know what the other is all about. Human beings don't think that inanimate objects glorify (God), yet those unmoving things are the most skilled worshippers of all!

Mathnawi III, 1490–1497

Never Stop Drinking the Water of Life

By God, never let yourself be satisfied with (the insight) you've gained; instead, always seek for more like one whose thirst can never be quenched. This noble gathering is eternal. Leave the place of honor behind and let the path (toward enlightenment) be your place of honor.

Mathnawi III, 1960–1961

Setting the Soul Free

Part of the realization that brings tranquility to the heart is the acceptance of the end of all things, even our own selves. The soul that stares into the face of its own death and walks away smiling is the one that truly achieves success. Why should a soul fear its end, unless it doesn't know where it's going? That essential knowledge is what awakening the soul is all about. There is life for the soul beyond death. We're not able to soar in spiritual ecstasy in this life for nothing. A plant is built to drink water; thus, water must exist for it. The human being has a consciousness that is above and beyond the mere material flesh of his or her body; thus, a conduit for that restless spirit exists, also.

In Rumi's understanding, the soul exists because of the love of God. The soul is a reflection of God's glory. Further still, the soul is made from the same kind of spirit-material as God Himself. God loaned our animal bodies this soul from Him. We spend all of our lives hearing the echoes of God in our heart. The yearning for meaning, the love for justice, the shame of evil—all of these things are evidence of a loftier potential. Our life's actions and beliefs influence, shape, and mold that soul within us, resulting in our own unique personality.

Rumi's References

Rumi was a strong exponent of the theory that our ability to experience spirituality was evidence of the existence of God, the source of spirituality. He wrote: "The Light is hidden, and the search is evidence in itself of its existence, for the heart doesn't seek safety for nothing. If the prison of this world offered no place of sanctuary, then there would never have been any feelings of aversion for it, nor would the heart seek a release from it."

—Mathnawi IV, 2037–2038

The goal of all religions is to purify the soul of our fleshly desires and base motivations. When death releases our inner energy—our very souls—back into the great beyond, we merely return to the One Who loaned us our essence in the first place. Like metal to a magnet, our essence must return to its Source. Thus, Rumi would argue, the only one who need fear death is the one who left his soul to whither, while the one who is free from the fear of death is the one who polished his soul so clearly that it reflects the glory of God, and thus is ready to rejoin Him in eternity. Let's read Rumi's thoughts on this subject.

We Were Made to Seek

You cannot sit still, even for a moment, without bringing something good or bad from yourself. This craving to always be active was instilled within you so that your inner consciousness could be made apparent by your outward behavior.

How can the body sit still, when like a fishing reel, it's constantly being tugged by the heart? The evidence of that pulling is your despair. Being inactive is worse than death to you.

Mathnawi II, 996–999

This World Is a Dream

This world is a passing dream—think nothing more of it than that. If you lose your hand in a dream, you're not really hurt. If you lose your head in a dream, not only is your head still there, but you'll keep on living long after that.

If you see yourself in a dream being cut in half—your body is normal when you wake up having no blemish at all! It all comes down to this: the body is never harmed in a dream whether from wounding or being pulverized into 200 pieces!

The Prophet said that this world, which seems so real, is no more than a sleeper's dream. You've accepted this idea at face value, but those who (truly realize that they're merely) passing through (this world), have already seen this, even without the Prophet's statement.

Mathnawi III, 1729–1734

Why Should I Fear?

Death took me from an inorganic state and endowed me with the growth of a plant. Then I died to organic plant growth and rose to the state of an animal.

Death then took me from the animal state and I became Adam! So why should I be afraid of another death? When did I ever become less from the act of dying?

In the next stage, I'm going to die as a human, so I can soar high above and raise my head among the angels. I'll have to leap out of that river of angelic being, as well, for everything will pass away save for His Face.

Mathnawi III, 3901–3904

def•i•ni•tion

The ideal of the Sufi path is to achieve union with the Divine even before death calls the soul back to God. This is often expressed in the term *fana,* which means annihilation. The idea is to give up desire for this world in order to make one's self desire only Him. Thus, one loses his soul in God, which was his original home to begin with.

Parting Words from Life

On the day when I've died, and while my coffin is yet passing by, think not that I feel any pain at leaving this world.

Cry not for me, and don't say, "O how awful! O how sad!" for then you'll fall into the error of Satan, and that would be truly tragic indeed!

When you attend my funeral, don't say, "Parting and separation," for that will be my time of union and meeting (with God).

When you lower me into the grave, don't say, "Peace be unto you! Good-bye!" for the grave is only a veil for concealing the gathering of souls in Paradise.

When you see the coffin being lowered down, be sure to notice the soul rising up. Why should there be any loss on account of the setting of the sun and moon?

It may seem like a setting to you, but for me it's a new dawn. The grave may seem like a prison, but for me it's the liberation of the soul.

What seed ever sunk into the earth that didn't sprout back to life again? Therefore, why is there this doubt for you about the human "seed"?

What bucket ever went down that didn't come back up full? Why should there be any mourning for the Joseph of the soul on account of the well?

When you've closed your mouth on this side, open it on that side, for your cries of joy will be in the heavens beyond both place and time.

From the *Divan*

The Least You Need to Know

- ◆ Rumi believed that God is the source for all love. The purpose of life is to unlock that love, make it a part of your soul, and then to live each day to the fullest in expectation of something better in the life beyond.

- ◆ People can achieve inner tranquility when they rely more upon God's plan and less upon their own hopes, fears, and uncertain circumstances.

- ◆ The highest form of religious faith is to love God for His sake alone, and not for how much He will reward you for it.

- ◆ Fear of death can be overcome through spiritual mastery of the inner soul. Rumi spent his life in this pursuit and died in exultant expectation of union with the Divine.

Chapter 9

Celebrating Earthly Passion

In This Chapter

- ◆ How Rumi expressed his lofty affection for all living things in human terms

- ◆ Some of Rumi's most treasured poems on love

- ◆ How earthly passion is a reflection of our longing for the Divine

- ◆ Rumi's views on what constitutes true love—and loss

Rumi was a passionate advocate for sincerity to one's inner self. For Rumi, to be at peace within one's soul was to gain a lasting treasure of untold value. Beyond the secrets of spiritual mastery, however, he was also a man of great affection and understanding toward his students, friends, and family. His capacity for human love and emotion was another facet of his expansive personality, so it may come as no surprise that Rumi also wrote extensively on the phenomenon of earthly love and passion. Indeed, his poems of love, desire, and loss are among the finest examples of the genre that any author has ever produced.

In this chapter, we'll embark upon a journey through this passionate facet of Rumi's writing talent. Most of the following selections you'll find are taken from the *Rubaiyat* portion of the *Divan*, the work that focuses the most on matters of emotional intelligence and depth. In the end, I think you'll agree that in addition to being a master of the soul, Rumi also knew how to speak from the heart.

Yearning for Love

Sometimes the greatest inspiration for awakening a slumbering heart comes from a desire to find love. When the heart becomes aware of its own emptiness, a fire is set ablaze inside that bangs on every wall and kicks open every door in its frantic search to let the light of love in. When the eye transmits the image of an ideal mate to the burning heart, all the resources of the mind and body are directed toward the pursuit of the beloved. The lofty yearning of the heart to find its soul-mate and earthly companion is a power not to be denied. How many are the star-crossed lovers who saw the object of their desire and earnestly pursued it? Rumi knew this kind of love and pain well. In these following selections, you'll see how beautifully Rumi expresses this yearning for a beloved.

The Power of Passion

Passion makes old medicine fresh. Passion lops off the flimsy branch. Passion is the remedy that refreshes; how can there be exhaustion when passion is there? Moan longingly no more from weariness: seek passion, passion, passion!

Mathnawi VI, 4302–4304

What Madness Is Love

The pretty one whispers under her breath, and you go crazy, senseless—you have no reason left! O Lord, what kind of spell is this, what kind of magic weaves its charm on even a heart of stone?

From the *Divan*

Love Bewilders All

I swear that ever since I've seen your face, this world's become a sham, a dream-like place. This garden has become so confused. What's a leaf? What's a blossom? It knows not this or that! Baffled birds cannot tell even a seed from a trap!

From the *Divan*

Footprints of the Master

Sufi poetry is often filled with allusions to wine, beloved ones, madness, and other seemingly bawdy things. The reality is that Sufis use such allusions as a metaphor for the kind of giddy feeling one gets when one begins to get in touch with spirituality on an ever-deeper level.

Don't Go

If you feel any longing for me, then say so.
If you live without love, alone, I want to know.
If your heart holds a place for me, then reveal it.
Tell me if it's so, or just tell me no, but be honest.

From the *Divan*

Love at First Sight

I swear by the heart that lies humbled before her; I swear by the soul that's drunk on her wine; I swear by that moment when I first saw her, a cup in one hand, and her hand in mine.

From the *Divan*

Lose Yourself in Love

Now that your lover has shown you her face, lose yourself at her feet, O my heart. Snuff out this candle that burns before the sun, for this heartache will die even as you will, so groan no more in pain.

From the *Divan*

Love Is More Than Skin Deep

Whoever is loved is beautiful; that doesn't mean that all those who are beautiful are loved. People used to say to Majnun, "There are plenty of girls more beautiful than Layla. Let us present them to you." Majnun used to answer them, "I'm not in love with Layla merely for her form. Layla is like a cup in my hand. I drink sweetness from that cup. I'm in love with that flavor. You only see the cup and are heedless of the drink it contains. A golden cup studded with gems, what use is that to me if all it holds is vinegar? An old broken gourd that's filled with delicious sweetness is better for me than 100 cups of gold."

From the *Fihi Ma Fihi*

Waiting for Your Love

How long will I remain roasting in your flame?
How long will you continue to turn me away?
How many friends will abandon me in shame?
How long will I feel this pain?

How long will you go on living without me?

From the *Divan*

Don't Turn Me Away

If I wasn't so pathetically in love with you, I wouldn't be standing here at your door. Don't tell me, "Go away. Get away from my door!" I wouldn't exist, my dear, if it wasn't for me standing here.

From the *Divan*

I Suffer for Your Love

I took a journey through the desert of your love, vainly searching for some sign that you might join me.

I peered in every house, as I passed along the way, seeing only the scattered remnants of those who traveled here before, and whom you cast away.

From the *Divan*

A page from a commentary on the Mathnawi *written in Persian by Mir Ali, c. 1514.*

The Power of Love

Through love, that which is bitter is made sweet.

Through love, copper is turned into gold.

Through love, what is muddled becomes clear.

Through love, pain becomes a source of healing.

Through love, the dead are raised to life.

Through love, kings are turned into slaves.

This kind of love is learned, for when did a simpleton ever sit upon such a throne?

Mathnawi II, 1529–1532

The Joys of Love Unfettered

When the quest for the beloved has reached its fulfillment, and the object of desire has consented to let the star-struck lover into its dazzling new home, then a new world appears on the horizon—a garden of joy and perpetual bliss, enwrapped within the arms of safety and union! Rumi revels in this feeling of love offered and reciprocated. As you read the next selection of his poems, see if you can catch a glimpse of him laughing in his garden with his beloved.

How Does It Feel to Be in Love?

This is what love is like: to fly toward a secret sky, to cause 100 veils to fall in a single moment, to give up your very life. Love is taking a step without feet, to look upon everything in the world as invisible, and to lose all recollection of who you are inside.

From the *Divan*

Wisdom of the Ages

Muslim civilization has produced an enormous number of poets. One of these, whose work influenced Rumi, was a woman named Rabi'ah al-Adawiyya (d. 801). She once wrote, "Eyes are at rest, the stars are setting. Hushed are the stirrings of birds in their nests and of monsters in the sea. You are the Just Who knows no change, the Balance Who can never swerve, the Eternal Who never passes away. The doors of kings are bolted now and guarded by soldiers. Your door is open to all who would call upon You. Each love, my Lord, is now alone with his beloved, and now I am alone with You."

What Love Said to Me

Love whispered in my ear, "To be chased is better than to be a hunter. Become my fool—let me swindle you. Give up the glorious sun and become a speck of dust. Live outside my door and become homeless. Don't pretend to be a candle; rather, be the moth that you are so you can taste the sweet flavor of life and lose yourself in thoughts of the majesty of slavery (to love)."

Mathnawi V, 411–414

Wonderstruck in Love

A rare prize has come my way; oh, what should I do?

She's left my mind in such a daze; oh, what should I do? Sometimes I feel like such a hypocrite and a fraud! When beauty gives you a kiss such as this, oh my, what's a holy man to do?

From the *Divan*

The Treasure of a Kiss

Look at her with her raven-colored hair. Look at the grace with which she holds herself there. Think of the sweetness of those ruby-red lips. "Charity for a kiss," I begged her, "for God's sake grant me this." "Oh my," she smiled and laughed my way, "Just imagine the gains you'd make from that exchange today!"

From the *Divan*

Loving More Than Just Her Good Side

There's more to her beauty than her laughter and her face. Her anger, her moods, her harsh words are all pretty, too. Whether I like it or not, she asks me for my soul. What do I care for my life? What she wants from me is lovely, too!

From the *Divan*

Challenge Me

I want a lover who will challenge me—a fighter, a brawler, a heart ablaze—someone who will argue with the sky and wrestle with destiny, who will burn like fire on a raging sea.

From the *Divan*

All I See Is You

I know when my heart begins to speak, it will end up humiliated in shame, fixated as it is on the image of your beauty; your face appears in every breath my heart takes.

From the *Divan*

Rumi's References _____

Rumi was influenced by the dramatic poetry of a writer named Ahmad al-Mutanabbi (d. 965). Here is a line from the *Diwan* of al-Mutanabbi that Rumi might have had memorized: "Grave harm have lovers done, loving before their life's begun."

The Expression of Love

Love united in life is expressed through physical joy and companionship. Two lovers on the cusp of union sing beautiful songs together. In his own subtle way, Rumi captured the essence of such times in a snapshot of scattered vignettes. Read on and entertain the romantic nature of Rumi's poetry of love as it unfolds.

Lovers Were Made for Each Other

There's a window between one heart and another; they're not separate or far from each other, like two different bodies. Two lamp stands may not be joined together, yet their light mingles as one as it passes beyond them.

No lover pursues his lover without his lover also pursuing him. This kind of passion from a lover makes the body as thin as a bowstring, yet the one who is loved like this appears beautiful and healthy. When the flash of love for a beloved shoots into a heart like this, then know that love dwells within that heart.

Mathnawi III, 4391–4395

Love Has Its Own Logic

The scholar is always showing off; the lover is always getting lost. A scholar always runs and hides in fear of drowning. Yet, the sole purpose of love is to drown in the sea!

Scholars plan for their retirement; lovers are ashamed to rest. Lovers are always alone, even when surrounded by a crowd. Just as water and oil don't mix, the lover remains apart from everyone.

The man who goes out of his way to give advice to a lover gets nothing in return. He leaves in ridicule, mocked by passion. Love is like musk; it always attracts attention. Love is like a tree, and lovers are its shade.

From the *Divan*

Finally Alone

My heart's happy tonight; I'm finally alone with my lover. At last, I'm free of the pain of our separation this night. As I dance with my lover, I pray in my heart, "Oh Lord, may the keys of the morning be forever lost tonight."

From the *Divan*

So Generous in Love

When I asked for just one kiss, you gave me six.

Where's the teacher who taught you that? Who's the one who trained you so well? You're so filled with goodness, so pure and so fine; you must've set the world free at least 1000 times!

From the *Divan*

Surprise

I made a suggestion softly in the ear of your playful heart. I shut my mouth and spoke to you in 100 silent ways. You know what I'm thinking; you've heard my every thought. Now I'm going to do tonight what I said I would before we were apart.

From the *Divan*

On Separation

Part of the risk of love is the potential pain of loss. If the rewards of love weren't so great, few would hazard such a gamble. Indeed, heartbreak is as much a part of the human experience as love. Where there is light, darkness lurks. Where there is passion, shattered dreams ring the edges like thorns on a rosebush. Rumi felt loss several times in his life; he knew what misery and sorrow felt like. His homeland, the city of his birth, was razed to the ground by the Mongols. His first wife, whom he loved dearly, passed away before him. His best friend, Shamsuddin of Tabriz, left him, returned, and then mysteriously disappeared. Rumi felt the pain of separation and loss in each of these instances. Let's explore poems that Rumi penned dealing with the subject of grief over lost love.

You Are My World

Out of everyone in all the world, I choose you. So will you now leave me to sit in sadness all alone? My heart is like a pen in your hand; you're the reason for my joy and sorrow. Except for what you want, what else can I have? Except for what you reveal, what more can I see?

You bring out both the thorn and the rose from within me. Sometimes I smell of roses; other times I'm snagged by thorns. In whatever way you keep me, that's how I will remain. Whatever you would make of me, that's what I will be.

In this body where you give color to the soul, who am I by myself? What is love and hate to me? You were the first to me, and you'll be the last. Make my ending better than my start!

When you're hidden from me, I lose all faith; when you're before me, I believe. I have nothing unless you gave it to me; what do you want from my heart and sleeve?

From the *Divan*

Wisdom of the Ages

Rumi wrote these lines in praise of love in his *Divan*: "Praise Love, Praise Love, for Love is divine and tender. Love is a beautiful thing, and oh so harmless. What passion, what passion, we're burning like the sun. It's hidden and obscure. That's an obvious sign."

Bring Me Joy Still

Even if all the rest leave me, my love, don't you go.

O friend, who drinks my sadness away, don't you go.

Fill my cup with mirth, and the sweet sound of your laughter. Please, good cupbearer, who lights up the world, don't you go away, too.

From the *Divan*

Loss

My moon, without you I weep like a rain cloud. Without you, I'm wounded, broken, and lonely. Banished from life, I sit here, alone, without you. I'm dying of shame, for my life has become empty since you've gone.

From the *Divan*

The Burning of a Broken Heart

You could stitch together 100 endless days,

Still my soul would find no release from this pain.

Do you laugh at these my words? Though you may know many things, you've never learned to love till you've gone insane.

From the *Divan*

Think No More of Me

If I die in this fight, in this battle with you,

I'll utter not a sigh, for fear of troubling you.

I'll die with a smile on my face, like a flower in your hand, from the wound that you made when you cut me away.

From the *Divan*

Life No More

Living is a sin without you. What kind of life can I lead without you there? Light of my life, each moment of life I pass without you is death. That's all the living that's left for me.

From the *Divan*

Let No Other In

God forbid your heart from entering another home, or growing distant from me when you're far from mine. Only your stream has fed my eyes as they blossomed. You're the source of my tears and my heart's sole passion.

From the *Divan*

Tears I Shed for You

I'll take hold of your feet; I won't let you leave.

Your love has caused a pain in my heart—who else but you can cure me? You tease me, telling me my heart has run dry. If that's true, then why does it flow now from my eyes?

From the *Divan*

Ruin

The many tears your loss has drawn from me can satisfy none, save my worst enemy. O you who are the center of my world, the pain of your going has broken my heart without yours even knowing what you've torn apart.

From the *Divan*

Solitude

She's left me. I never had such a friend like her. She left before my heart was full, or ready for an end like this. She's left me, and taken with her the only cure for this kind of pain. The rose has gone, and look—only the thorns remain.

From the *Divan*

Pain Has a Purpose

When God wants to help us (out of our distress), He turns our thoughts toward humble supplication. Oh, joy to the eye that weeps for His sake! Every sorrow eventually will end in laughter; the one who sees the end is a blessed servant indeed. Wherever there is flowing water, there is new life in the making. Wherever there are tears, the mercy of God will soon appear.

Mathnawi I, 817–820

Love Celebrated

Rumi was at his best when he spoke to the hearts of his listeners. Although the *Divan* contains many poems dedicated to the memory of his lost friend, Shamsuddin of Tabriz, the bulk of this book is an amalgamation of his early works on all subjects. Because his love poetry is so expressive and sincere, it's among the most popular of his entire repertoire. Here we will close with a few more selections on love and its beauty. Truly, Rumi was a master of both the soul and the heart.

The Story of Love

After I heard my first love story, I went out in search of you. I never understood how dark the road would be, for lovers don't find each other on the road somewhere; they're with each other all along.

From the *Divan*

Content in Love

When that beauty first stole my heart from me, my neighbors suffered every night from my constant weeping. Now that my love has grown and matured, my weeping has ceased. Isn't it the case that the fire that gets more air gives off less smoke?

From the *Divan*

Eternal Love

Even if you jabbed thorns into these weeping eyes, or shot cruel arrows at this flimsy heart, or beat on me like a drum and then beat on me some more, still I would never let you go. No, not even then.

From the *Divan*

 Footprints of the Master _____

Many devoted followers of Rumi perform their moving meditation exercises, or *sema'* rituals, accompanied by musicians playing hand drums, flutes, and stringed instruments.

Mutual Desire

God instilled desire in both men and women so that, by their union, the world could be maintained.

Mathnawi III, 4415

No Escape from Love

Once I said to myself, "I'll leave for a while. That will make my love miss me all the more." She had an endless amount of patience, though, and I couldn't hide for long. I never could make my plan work, no matter how many times I tried.

From the *Divan*

Indescribable

I wrote a poem, and my love got angry, either at me or at the poor quality of my rhymes. I said to her, "So why don't you tell me what to write?" She replied, "Why don't you tell me what poem could ever contain one such as I!"

From the *Divan*

School of Love

My heart is your student; it's a student of love.

Like the night, it waits by the gates of dawn.

Wherever I go, I follow where the face of love leads, for oil flows steadily toward the flame that it feeds.

From the *Divan*

Unforgettable

When I've steeped in the fire of my mind for a while, I think of forgetting you for some time so I can collect my soul and think about something else. Then you pour yourself back into my cup once more and once more, I go on drinking.

From the *Divan*

The Least You Need to Know

◆ Rumi wrote passionate poetry about love and the joy of being in love here on earth.

◆ Rumi's book, the *Divan*, is where the vast majority of his love poetry can be found.

◆ Rumi understood well the pain of losing a beloved, and this was precisely the main idea behind his *Divan* collection.

Part 4

In the Garden of Eternal Delight

Generations have been fascinated with Rumi's insight and unmatched storytelling skills. In this final part, take a journey through some of Rumi's more famous fables, with animals and clever imagination, and see for yourself what pleasantries can be had at his table, and the timeless wisdom he imparts.

Chapter 10

Wisdom to Live By

In This Chapter

◆ Discovering some of Rumi's practical advice for living an honest and worry-free life

◆ Understanding why Rumi placed so much emphasis on personal integrity

◆ Exploring what Rumi had to say about prayer and supplication and how they relate to daily life

◆ Enjoying Rumi's wry sense of the meaning of life and how to find useful wisdom within it

Rumi was a man of great depth. On that, there is no disagreement, but Rumi wasn't just a philosopher thinking profound thoughts on lofty topics. While it's easy to get that impression, given that the bulk of his translated works concern very weighty themes, in reality he wrote about a whole host of different subject matters. From his *Divan* we learn about his passion for love and about his humane disposition. On the other hand, his many collected sermons reveal a practical scholar eager to convince his audience of the necessity to be moral and high-minded through logical arguments based on the tangible benefits of personal and social harmony. Finally, his *Mathnawi* presents a whole host of different thoughts and ideas on morality, philosophy, and even good personal habits and manners—not just on matters connected to self-awareness.

Rumi was part of a living tradition whose values were rooted in long-standing mores and customs. He lived those precepts to the fullest and came up with ingenious ways to impart this lifestyle advice to others. Whether the subject is the practicality of hard work or the value of honesty, Rumi had much to say on these and other topics. In this chapter, we're going to take a wide look at these aspects of Rumi's teaching and explore his wisdom for daily living. You'll be surprised at how he tackles many of these issues, and perhaps you'll find much to apply in your own life.

Principles of Dignified Living

There are many ways a person can lead her life that are wholly unconnected with her material existence. If you put aside status, fashion, education, appearance, relationships, interests, and all the rest, leaving only you and your basic attitude and demeanor, what would you be like? What would you think of yourself? Do you think you might find something you would like to improve? A dignified life involves self-improvement and nobility of character. If we take no interest in improving our personality and habits, then what other advancements are we holding back as well? How can we learn to be more aware of our own shortcomings, especially when seeing our own faults is perhaps the hardest thing to do? The starting place is getting used to examining our own habits and personality closely. Rumi wrote extensively on this issue, and what follows is a brief passage through some of those areas in which Rumi advised we take particular care. Rumi advised this:

> Perhaps someone else sees faults within me that I don't see myself. For the one who recognizes his own faults before seeing them in others, how can he be so unconcerned about correcting himself? Most people don't pay attention to themselves, so they go on blaming each other!

Mathnawi II, 880–882

Shortcomings Cannot Remain Hidden

The odor of pride, greed, and lust is like the smell of onions (on the breath). Even though you swear that you haven't taken on any of those traits, saying, "I've never eaten any onions or garlic," still, the smell from your mouth as you make that oath betrays you, and repulses the noses of those who sit near you.

Many are the prayers that are rejected because of the bad smell (coming from a person's nature), for a corrupt heart shows on the tongue. The response to such a tainted prayer is no less than, "Get out of here!" for the reward of scoundrels is the hammer of repulsion. On the other hand, if the words of prayer are riddled with mistakes, but the intention is good, then such clumsy words are acceptable to God.

Mathnawi III, 166–171

Footprints of the Master

In classical times, an applicant to join the Mevlevi Sufi Order was first required to meet with a *Shaykh* who would try to talk him out of it. If the applicant persisted and remained quietly for three days sitting outside the kitchen door of the Sufi lodge, he would once again be asked to reconsider. If he still had his heart set on becoming a dervish, he would then spend the next 1,001 days working as a servant in the kitchen. If he ever showed any disobedience or refusal to adapt to his many menial duties, he would be asked to leave forever. If he completed his period of service, he would be given a *tenure*, or a dervish cloak, and would be a confirmed member of the Order ready to begin his higher studies.

How Arrogance Can Be Recognized

What is arrogance? It's being unconcerned about gaining what you really need, just as ice is ignorant of the sun. When ice finally realizes the sun is there, it has little chance to remain, for it softens, melts, and flows away.

Mathnawi V, 1941–1942

Do Not Overemphasize the Self

I'm the source of so much rot and idiocy, that no one, because of me, can live his life happily. I shout at everyone I see, and they, in turn, shout back at me. I cry for justice as you can see, yet, who can hope for it from me?

From the *Divan*

How Conceit Can Be Our Undoing

There once was a poor man who, because of his poverty, had a lowly reputation. In time, he began to grease his moustache in the morning with the fat of a sheep's tail. Thereafter he would go among the rich and say, "I was at a party and had a sumptuous feast." Then he would happily point to his moustache indicating that he wanted people to look at it, as if to say, "Look at this, for it's the proof that my words are true; here's the evidence that I've eaten greasy and expensive food."

However, his (hungry) stomach used to curse him silently, "May God unravel the schemes of liars! Your boasting is giving me heartburn. May your greasy moustache be torn away! You worthless boaster, if it wasn't for your deception, some wealthy person might have taken pity on me. If only you would have shown your sickness, and not been a faker, then some doctor could have found a cure (for your hunger)."

Thus, his stomach made supplications against his moustache, for it had no other avenue than prayer, saying, "O God, expose this lazy low-born scum, so that the noble may show pity on me." Soon enough, the stomach's prayer was answered. The urgency of the need raised a flag for aid. Didn't God promise: "Whether you're a scoundrel or an idolater, I'll answer when you call upon Me"? So be devoted to prayer and always cry out to God, for in the end it may save you from the hands of a phantom.

When the stomach commended itself to God's will, the cat came and carried away the sheep's tail. Even though they chased after her, the cat got away. The child of the boastful man turned pale at the thought of the punishment he would receive for not preventing the theft, but nevertheless, the little boy came in the midst of a gathering and destroyed his father's reputation.

"Father," he said, "the sheep's tail that you use to grease your moustache every morning is gone. The cat came and snatched it away. I ran after it, but I couldn't catch it."

Those who were there laughed in amazement and their feelings of pity were aroused. They invited the man to eat and thereafter they kept him well fed; they planted the seed of compassion in his soil. Now as for the poor man, after having tasted the nobility of the high-minded, he humbly devoted himself to honesty ever after.

Mathnawi III, condensed from 732–765

Wisdom of the Ages

Rumi advised us to avoid feeling offended by events around us in these words from the *Divan*: "A few flies were fighting over sugar as if it were a treasure. Why should the sugar care? A bird alighted on a mountain, rested, and then flew off again. Was the mountain made better or worse by that?"

Don't Put Off Remorse

Be warned! Don't commit a crime while taking refuge in the thought, "I can repent of it later on and be safe."

True repentance requires a flash (of realization) in the heart that's followed by a flood of tears. That kind of lightning flash and rain cloud is a prerequisite for sincere repentance.

Fruit needs a flash of lightning and the resultant rainfall to grow; therefore, rain clouds and lightening are an essential component to growth.

Unless there's a flash of lightning in the heart and streaming rain clouds in the eyes, how can the fire of God's anger be cooled? How can the lush growth of joyous union with God flourish, and how can clear fountains of spirit ever hope to gush forth again?

Mathnawi II, 1652–1656

It's often been said that a person should live with no regrets. Too many people allow regret to pile up inside by assuming they can reform themselves at a later date. They put off the task of examining their inner self, their morals, their motivations, and the needs of their soul until most of their life is gone. Rumi warns us of this in these words:

> Some people rely on the promise of "Tomorrow," and they wander for years around that door, yet "Tomorrow" never comes. A long time has to pass for a person's inner self to become purified—indeed, some matters take longer than others. Only then can you know if there's a treasure buried under the surface of your body, or whether a snake or an ant or a dragon dwells within. By the time a person finds out that he's in need of repair, the life of the seeker may have come near its end, and what use would his knowledge of his inner self be then?

> *Mathnawi* I, 2279–2282

As Rumi advises, don't put off self-reformation for some mythical "Tomorrow," or do wrong today in the expectation that you will have time later to fix it. If a wrong does happen, be quick to make amends. How many are those who have left this life filled with unresolved regrets and wrongs committed against others! No matter how much a person's consciousness is filled with remorse, he cannot always fix events that occurred long before in his youth, and the overwhelming sense of futility we may experience in the future is not worth the momentary gain today.

def•i•ni•tion

The word for repentance among Sufis is **tawbah**. This is an Arabic word that means to return to God seeking humble forgiveness.

Don't Covet the World

Rumi was very hard on greed. He understood greed to be the desire to obtain material goods or worldly honors in excess of what one needs. For Rumi, trying to build your fortune around the baubles of the world is like trying to hold on to a fistful of sand. Though you may thrust your hands into the beach and say, "This is mine," yet how will you hold it when the tide sweeps it away? In reality, nothing you covet in this world is worth a single grain of dust in the great scheme of things. Rumi explained it this way:

> Wealth has no permanence: it comes in the morning, and at night, it scatters away. Attractiveness has no real importance, for a beautiful face can gain a yellow scar from a thorn scratch.
>
> A noble lineage is also not worth very much, for the noble-born can be made the fool by money and fancy horses. Oh, how many a nobleman's son has disgraced his father through wanton mischief and shameful deeds!
>
> *Mathnawi* VI, 255–258

Avoid the Company of Fools

Rumi strongly advised people to remove themselves from the company of those who behave in a heedless and foolish manner. He wrote this:

> Run away from the foolish, for even Jesus fled from them. Oh, how much blood has been shed by keeping fools as friends!
>
> The air makes the water evaporate slowly, and in the same way, a fool steals your faith away from you. He draws away your heat and gives you frost in exchange, as if someone put hard stones under your seat.
>
> Jesus didn't run away (from fools) because he was afraid of them; he wanted to teach us by his example.
>
> *Mathnawi* III, 2595–2558

Without a doubt, we're influenced by those whom we choose to keep in our circle. Rumi understood well that this could be a blessing or a curse. Think about what you would like to get out of life. What are your hopes, your plans, and your dreams? Are those around you a help or a hindrance to achieving your goals? Do those around you bring out the best or worst in you? If you find that someone is a slow drag on your very life essence, what are you waiting for? Why suffer the slow death of a thousand cuts? Would you let a thief steal money away from you, as long as it was only a few dollars a day? Do you only notice the big thefts that rob you of your happiness and ignore the slow, steady draining of someone who sees you as no more than an easy dupe?

Rumi's reference to Jesus reminds us that Jesus did not suffer the fools of the temple; he threw the money changers out and kept them away from the holy places he wanted to frequent. Learning from this, consider what sort of housecleaning you should do in your own life.

Two Personal Habits for Success

There are many Sufi principles and practices that dervishes have used, tested, and honed for countless centuries to help them on their spiritual journeys, and these same practices can be found in nearly all other religions of the world. This is no surprise when we remember, as we discussed in Chapter 2, that the basic premise of Islam (Rumi's religion) is that all true religions began with an authentic prophet from God. Therefore, to find similar techniques for spiritual growth among them all is to be expected. Among the practices common to all and most praised by Rumi were supplication and wrestling with hunger. To him, they were two key exercises for gaining greater focus and self-mastery.

Be Not Too Proud to Ask for Help

Supplication is an essential part of maintaining a healthy inner spirit. Whether one believes in a Supernatural Power or not, the very act of giving voice to what one needs is both therapeutic and affirming. In other words, a person may have a vague idea that she wants to solve some problem in her life, but it may never become a clearly defined goal in her subconscious mind. This may cause a delay in planning and striving toward its fulfillment. In other words, unless a person's focus is an actually articulated gesture, she may suffer from a vague sense of unfulfilled tasks.

def•i•ni•tion

Supplication is the act of making a humble appeal to the one who has the power to grant a request of yours.

Supplication also serves another purpose, and that is in the area of reassurance and stress reduction. Even more than defining goals in the traditional sense, if we feel overwhelmed or in a state of loss, the mere act of asking for assistance can motivate the mind to seek solutions. What can be said, however, to those who feel that their supplications remain unanswered? As Rumi explains, the fault is not in the lack of an answer, but rather our inability to see the solution when it comes to us. This is what he wrote:

> One night a man was crying, "O God!" until his lips were primed with His sweet praise.
>
> Then Satan whispered in his mind, "And so, O you talkative one, where is the reply that says, 'Here I am,' to all your cries of 'God'? You haven't received a single answer from the Throne. How long will you keep crying 'God' with a sour face?"
>
> The man became filled with despair, and he went to bed gloomily. Soon he saw a saint named Khidr in a dream, sitting among fields of green, and the saint said, "You there! Why have you stopped uttering your praises of God? Why are you wishing that you never called upon Him?"
>
> The man replied to Khidr in his dream, saying, "I haven't heard any sounds of 'Here I am,' in answer, so I'm afraid that I've been turned away from the door (of God's mercy)."
>
> Khidr answered the man, saying, "Not so! God says that your very saying of 'God' implies the answer of 'Here I am,' and that your supplication, sorrow, and perseverance is My reply to you. Your fear and love is the net to catch My mercy. Underneath every, 'O Lord' of yours is a 'Here I am' of Mine."

Mathnawi III, 189–197

Rumi's References

Khidr is the name of a character that appears in Chapter 18 of the Qur'an. He was a wise man from whom the prophet Moses learned patience. This enigmatic figure is a prominent reference in Sufi literature as the archetype of the enlightened and perfect Shaykh.

Use the Body's Needs to Your Advantage

Hunger, which can mean many things, is more than just a byproduct of missing your routinely scheduled intake of food. Hunger is actually a very good teacher. Look at the cycle we all struggle with every day: we eat because we feel hungry, and we feel hungry because we live in a physical body. Because our body has needs, it often exaggerates those needs because it's afraid we may deprive it at some point. Therefore, the body works overtime to convince us to overindulge in whatever urges it feels at the moment. If the body has mastery over the will of a person, then that person is a slave to his or her body. By extension, that soul or spirit is then a second-class citizen in its own home.

Rumi advised us to gain mastery over our physical urges, and chief among them is our desire to eat. Now, Rumi never advocated that people should starve themselves. He merely called for people to allow themselves to experience hunger sometimes and to deny its call for a while as a way to practice physical self-control. He wrote this:

> Hunger is the greatest of all cures. Listen; learn the lessons of hunger; don't consider hunger to be a bad thing. Everything that's flavorless is made sweet with hunger. Without hunger, even the tastiest morsel will have no flavor.
>
> *Mathnawi* V, 2832–2833

We can all learn the lessons that fighting with hunger can teach. Rumi emphasized this by writing, "Fasting is the first principle of medicine; fast and see the strength of the spirit reveal itself." All religions teach some form of fasting for this very purpose. Even nonreligious self-improvement programs emphasize gaining mastery over the body's urges as a way to develop self-control, self-esteem, and good personal habits. It's not that we have to go on a diet, but rather that when we feel hungry we should sometimes try to put off eating for as long as possible so our stomach knows who the boss is. After a while it gets easier and easier to do. That simple act of willpower empowers us in all other areas of our life, as well, and it costs nearly nothing to do—just a simple, occasional delay. Rumi wrote this:

> O you, whose stomach is greedy, turn away (from the world), for the only way to change (yourself) is to change your diet.

O you whose heart is sick, turn toward the cure, for the only course of treatment is to change your outlook.

O you who are a prisoner to food, you'll only escape if you let yourself be weaned from it.

There's food enough for you in hunger! Look for it in earnest, and be ever hopeful (of finding it), O you who would diminish (your dependence on material things).

Feast yourself upon the light. Be like an eye that sees! Be one with the angels so you can be delivered from stress.

Mathnawi V, 293–298

Wisdom of the Ages

The twelfth-century scholar, Muhammad al-Ghazali (d. 1111), whose works influenced Rumi, wrote about the benefits of wrestling with hunger in this way: "Gain mastery over the body with the overseer of hunger."

Think about it: those who are hungry for food or anything else go out and pursue the object of their desire. Even if they don't attain it, their senses are heightened, their awareness of their surroundings peaks, and their cunning and precision get a workout. That greater exposure to the reality of life, from the experience of hunger, helps awaken the soul from its slumber. Thereafter it keeps the soul refreshed, for by denying the resolution of the body's urge to eat, you peak all your senses. It may be an unpopular idea at first, to actually deny your cravings once in a while, but the benefits will be innumerable. This is what Rumi said:

Be careful in how much you eat, for too much food can be a poison for you. Watching the diet is what brought strength and enlightenment to the prophets.

Mathnawi III, 214

Wise Principles to Live By

Now let us turn to some common sense advice from Rumi to guide you in your daily affairs. Ponder over how you can make use of these principles, and know that Rumi practiced and perfected each of these.

How to Judge a Person's Character

If through incomplete information you have no idea how a person is inside, look to whom he has made his leader, for every foal goes to its mother, and so by such association you can know for certain (what that person stands for).

Mathnawi IV, 1640–1641

Trust Your Feelings

Whenever a *good* person starts to feel some sense of lurking suspicion in the heart, it doesn't come without just cause. Consider that hint of wisdom to be among the attributes of divine providence, and not a mere misgiving. In that case, the inner light of the heart is seeing through the tablet of universal truth.

Mathnawi VI, 2743–2744

Truth Is the Catalyst for Tranquility

Given that truth, in all its brightness, is the essence of tranquility; likewise, the heart can never be calmed by false words. Falsehood is like having a piece of straw stuck in the mouth, which itself is like the heart. Straw never stays quietly hidden in the mouth. As long as it's there, the one who's annoyed by it keeps moving his tongue to get it out. Even worse than that is when a speck of straw is blown in the eye; it shuts itself tight and waters until it's gone.

Mathnawi VI, 2576–2579

Look for No Solutions in Violence

Violence is never the way to ward off hardship; rather, the method should be through generosity, forgiveness, and kindness.

Mathnawi VI, 2590–2591

A nineteenth-century drawing of a dervish whirling in the style that Rumi pioneered, chanting the praises of God.

The Law of Karma

If you've ever eaten too much honey, does the stomachache affect someone else? When you've worked for an entire day, does someone else get paid at the coming of night? Has there ever been any kind of effort on your part without its results coming back to you? Have you ever planted any seed without the harvest sprouting for you? Your actions, which arise from your soul's inclinations and your body's motivations, cling to your robe like your own child!

Mathnawi VI, 417–420

Don't Numb the Mind with Desires

People are distracted by their desires, and afterward they repent of all the forbidden things in which they indulged. In reality, such a person gratifies his lusts with nothing more than a phantom, and he ends up further away from the truth than he was before!

Your desire for fleeting pleasure is like having a wing that you could have used to fly up to the truth. Yet, whenever you indulge in forbidden things, your wing falls off and you become lame—moreover, the phantom of pleasure flees from you, as well!

Protect that wing and don't indulge in forbidden things, so that the wing of desire can carry you into Paradise. People who sin think they're having a good time, when in reality, they're tearing off their wings for the sake of an illusion.

Mathnawi III, 2133–2138

Bad Habits and Their Cure

Know that every one of your bad habits is a thorn bush; its thorns have been stuck in your foot many a time. How often have you been wounded by your own habits! Don't you have any sense? Perhaps you're without it!

If other people are wounded by what comes from within you, and you don't care, at least you'll notice it when you're wounded! In that case, you would be a source of pain to both yourself and everyone else around you!

Either take up an axe and chop like an adult (against your bad habits), or weave those thorns into a rosebush. Join the light of the Friend with the fire (of your shortcomings) so that by His light you can overwhelm your fire and through Him transform all your thorns into roses.

Mathnawi II, 1240–1246

A Wise Reminder

Rumi called upon us to remain ever-cognizant of the one, overriding fact of our brief existence—that material goods, no matter how many we acquire, bring no happiness in themselves. Rather, happiness comes from unlocking our real treasure within. All the many principles for good living that you've perused in this chapter, whether it's to practice supplication or to learn to trust your common sense, are merely an arrow pointing the way toward this all important understanding. Should a person go through life like a magnet passing through a junkyard? If she did, how much of the real person would be left at the end of the road? How does this compare to the one who learns to peel away those things that blot out her true self? Ponder over this and see how your own life stacks up on the climb toward eternal bliss. Listen to what Rumi was saying when he penned these words:

> Within each and every human being there's so much love, anguish, restlessness, and desire that even if he owned 100,000 planets, he would still find no rest or peace within them.
>
> People dedicate themselves to all kinds of occupations, crafts, and professions, becoming everything from astrologers to doctors; yet, none of them are at peace, for the very thing they all so desperately seek through their endeavors cannot be found there.
>
> The Beloved is called *the Satisfaction of the Soul* precisely because it's only through Him that the heart can find satisfaction. How can anything else provide peace then?
>
> All the various pleasures and pursuits of this world are like the parts of a ladder. The different steps on the ladder are not places to remain, but rather stages that must be passed through.
>
> The quicker someone wakes up and realizes this, the shorter the road becomes and the less time is wasted killing time on these intermediate steps.
>
> From the *Fihi Ma Fihi*

The Least You Need to Know

- Rumi's writings recommend both spiritual advancement and leading a good and honest life. He wrote extensively about the principles for wholesome living.

- Supplication is an excellent way to focus the mind and bring solace to the soul.

- When a person refrains from giving in to his feelings of hunger for at least a little while, he begins to master the art of self-control.

- Bad habits can be identified and eliminated from our daily lives by contemplating the effects of what we do and then reforming ourselves one habit at a time.

Chapter 11

Animal Fables

In This Chapter

- ◆ Some famous fables of Eastern folklore used by Rumi
- ◆ How Rumi altered existing fables to make spiritual statements
- ◆ The lessons of life Rumi hid within some of his more fantastic tales
- ◆ What Rumi had to say about the debate between destiny and free will

Every culture has produced a rich myriad of fables and animal tales to impart essential lessons and wisdom. In the West, tales from Aesop, Chaucer, and the Brothers Grimm still delight children and adults to this day. The mystics and poets of the East have also found such fables to be useful teaching methods and have liberally produced such stories in books ranging from the *Arabian Nights* to *The Conference of the Birds*. In fact, the lines between fact and fiction, realization and befuddlement, and truth and imagination are often riddled with the tracks of personified animals. Though people of a more rational frame of mind might be quick to dismiss the usage of animal characters for the teaching of wisdom, Rumi was quick to note otherwise.

Children tell their tales, but in their stories, there may be many a mystery and lesson to be learned. Even though in their tales they may relate a whole host of silly things, always look for treasures in such ruined places!"

Mathnawi III, 2602–2603

In this chapter, then, we'll journey through the most well-known and instructive of Rumi's animal fables. As you read each of them, try to envision the many different paths of wisdom contained within them. Perhaps you'll smile at the thought that many generations of Sufis and lay people have discussed these and other stories at length around the flickering light of a midnight fire. Though the stories cross the line of the rational into the imaginative, the lessons they impart are more real and poignant than meets the eye.

It All Depends on Your Vantage Point

In this tale, Rumi points out the foolishness of claiming exclusive truth. In the end, what one person may believe as true may be nothing more than his or her peculiar point of view. This is what Rumi wrote:

Every lamp is different, but all light is the same—it comes from another plane entirely. If you focus only upon the lamp, then you'll be lost, for the lamp brings out division and peculiarities. If you stay focused on the light, however, then you'll be saved from the divisions and peculiarities of the physical object. O you who are the seed of all being, the disagreement between the Muslim, Zoroastrian, and Jew merely depends on the point of view.

An elephant was in a darkened house; some Indians had brought it there for display. Soon, many people came to get a glimpse of it; they filed in one after another into the darkened room.

Now, because it was impossible to see anything with the eye in that dark place, each person used the palm of his hand to feel the elephant in the darkness (to gain a sense of what it was like).

One person's hand touched its trunk, causing him to say, "This animal is like a water-pipe." Another person's hand touched its ear, and he thought it was like a fan. Another person took hold

of its leg and said, "I think this elephant is shaped like a pillar."
Yet another person touched its back and said, "Undoubtedly, this
elephant is like a high throne."

In this way, whenever anyone heard a description of the elephant,
he understood it only in the context of the part he had touched.
Due to their differing points of view, their descriptions differed.
One man said it was crooked while another man said it was
straight!

If each of them had carried a candle in his hand, then their statements would not have been so diverse. Normal eyesight is like the
palm of the hand. The palm cannot touch the entire (picture) at
once. The eye that sees as broadly as a wide ocean is one thing,
while (the eye that can only see) the foam is another. Leave the
foam and look with the eye of an ocean.

Mathnawi III, 1256–1270

How often do we encounter situations in which we don't see the full
picture? How many stories have we heard without getting all the facts?
How many times have we pointed the finger at others, without realizing our own incomplete grasp over the affair, and when the same happens to us we cry out for understanding? In this world, we often form
our opinions by what we see, know, or experience, yet we are often
exposed to so little of the big picture. The wise person is the one who
is not so hasty to act or form opinions based on her own observations.
She instinctively realizes that there's more to every story than meets
the eye. The only way a person can ever hope to get a handle on the
larger truth is if she steps back and takes a wider look at what others
see. Only then does wisdom open the inner eye of the mind, enabling
us to see everything more clearly.

The Story of the Three Fish

Here is an aquatic tale that Rumi borrowed from an existing story collection he was familiar with called *Kalila and Dimnah*. Rumi put his
own spin on the account and drew out several spiritual lessons.

This is the story, O stubborn one, of a lake in which there were three huge fish. You've already seen it in *Kalila*, though that book only had the outer shell of this tale, while here you'll find the hidden meaning.

Three fishermen once passed by the edge of this lake; they saw that there was much prey contained within. Therefore, they hurried to bring their nets to bear.

The fish saw what the men were doing, and they knew what the men intended. The smartest fish decided to migrate, even though it would be a difficult and arduous journey.

"For sure," he said, "I'm not going to ask for advice from the others, for I'm certain that they'll try to weaken my resolve. They love their home too much, and their lethargy and ignorance might affect me, too."

This cautious fish then swam away on his belly, for he was leaving the home of danger and heading toward the sea of light. Thus, that fish departed and found his way into the sea. For him, he chose distance and a broad destination as his final goal.

Now when the second fish realized he was no longer under the protection of the smartest fish, and when he saw his hour of trial drawing near, he said, "He's gone to the sea and is now freed from his worries; my good friend has left me. But I won't dwell on that, for now I have to look after myself. I know—I'll pretend that I'm dead. I'll float belly-up on the surface of the water and act as if I had died. I'll make myself one with this water. To feign death before being made to die is to be safe from harm."

Wisdom of the Ages

In the story of the three fish, the first fish is a metaphor for the Sufi who abandons love of this life and withdraws from its concerns.

Therefore, the second fish feigned death in that way, and turned belly-up. The water then carried him on its current, sometimes bobbing on the surface, sometimes swirling below. When the fishermen saw this, they were distressed and cried out, "Oh no! The best fish is dead!"

The fish heard what they said and was elated. He thought to himself, "My trick worked, so now I'm safe from the knife." Then, one of the deserving fishermen took hold of him, spit on him in disgust, and threw him on the shore. (When the man turned his attention away,) this somewhat intelligent fish rolled over continuously until it finally slipped quietly back in the water and got away.

Meanwhile, the thoughtless third fish kept darting all around in apprehension and worry. That fool fish was jumping out of the water, leaping to the left and to the right, trying to save itself from the net by its own efforts. When the fishermen cast their nets, he was caught up in them. His own foolishness had secured a place for him in the fire of doom.

Soon there he was above a fire, lying flat in a frying pan. He had become the very companion of foolishness. While he was roasting in the flames, the voice of reason called out to him, saying, "Didn't any warning ever come to you?" Then, from the rack of torture and torment, he answered back, as the souls of the faithless (in Hell) will say, "Yes, indeed! Warning did come, and I remained heedless."

Mathnawi IV, condensed from lines 2202–2285

Rumi's References

Rumi sometimes borrowed stories from other sources and wove them in his narratives to make a point. Some of his animal tales were taken from the Arabic literary classic entitled *Kalila and Dimnah*, which was a collection of animal and people fables, also known as the *Pancha Tantra*. (Rumi always gave proper attribution!)

There are many ways of looking at life and many ways to live it. That in itself is no guarantee of safety. This is why everyone and everything from religious teachings and our parents to local laws and even our own conscience warn us to be cautious. Yet how many people listen? The dangers of unchecked material desires and pleasures are like a net that's ready to trap us and deliver us to ruin. The farsighted person learns to recognize the world for what it is, namely, as a trap for the heedless. Such a one chooses to withdraw from it, like the first fish in the story, and seek guaranteed safety.

The weak-willed, as represented by the second fish, compromise with the world and let the current carry them where it wills, hoping to somehow make it through and avoid the many pitfalls and dangers that lurk around every corner.

The heedless, represented by the third fish, go through life without any plan or understanding. They simply live in a happy-go-lucky fashion, until they panic whenever imminent danger suddenly rears its ugly head. But they have no way to escape from the net of their own making; they've damaged themselves with self-inflicted wounds and are too weak to wriggle away. As a result, they suffer from horrible trials and experience painful regret when the final realization hits them—that they were warned what would happen if they didn't wise up, and that now it's too late for them to save themselves. Think about which of the three fish Rumi would have praised and why.

The Foal Who Refused to Drink

Here is a short moral tale about a horse and her foal. In its handful of lines, it contains a powerful message stressing the importance of focus in daily living. Rumi wrote the following:

> A foal and her mother went to drink water in the barn, but when they arrived they found some stable boys there yelling at them, "Come on now! Drink it!"

> The noise of all that yelling bothered the foal, and she held up her head from the trough and refused to drink. Her mother asked, "My child, why are you refusing to drink this water?"

> The foal replied, "These humans are yelling, and I'm afraid of their shouting. My heart is trembling and shaking; I fear their shouting is directed at me."

> The mother horse answered, saying, "Ever since the world began, there have always been noisy loud-mouths like that on the earth."

> Get on with your own affair, O worthy one, for soon they'll tear out their beards in anguish. Time is running out, and the ample water is flowing away. Drink of it now, for if you're separated from it, you'll fall into pieces.

Mathnawi III, 4292–4300

Think of all the people you've known in your life who brought you nothing but noise—shouting, distracting, drama—all to get your attention and feed their own emptiness inside. If you hearken to them, you wind up losing one precious thing after another, and they can never repay you for your loss. Rumi counsels you to accept that there will always be people trying to distract you—it's the way of things from time immemorial. When you realize the noise cannot be stopped, then you can work on tuning it out so you can get on with the business of your life. The influence of busybodies and users holds us back, and it's only when we understand this that we can begin to learn how to work around them.

The Story of the Ferocious Lion

The following story, derived from *Kalila and Dimnah*, is one of the lengthier tales from the *Mathnawi*, weighing in at 490 verses. (Don't worry; it's presented here in a greatly condensed version without the many digressions.) What makes this tale important is that it tackles the issue of fate versus free will. Should people rely upon fate/destiny alone, or upon free will alone, or should they rely upon a combination of destiny and free will? This is an issue tackled by every religion and philosophy, and Rumi also gives us his take on the issue through this colorful and clever tale.

> There once was a valley full of animals who were used to being hunted. However, they were being harassed by a particularly aggressive lion of late.
>
> The lion kept jumping out to ambush them and carry them away, so much so that the pasturelands had become a danger to them all. (To save themselves from this fiend), the animals devised a plan.
>
> One day they approached the lion and said, "Let's make a deal. We'll make sure you're fed with a fixed amount of food every day, just so long as you don't venture out anymore to hunt, for the grass here has now become bitter for us."
>
> "I would like to agree," the lion replied, "as long as you hold up your end of the bargain and don't try to cheat me. I've been swindled many times by this one and that. Now I'm finished with the

tricks and lies of men, for I've been bitten by the sting of deceitful snakes and scorpions. Ah, but even worse than deceitful men and spite, however, is my gluttonous soul; it lies in ambush inside of me, (and it causes me to over-hunt in my greed. Should I ratify this agreement with you? I don't know,) for I once heard from the Prophet, 'A believer is never bitten from the same snake hole twice,' and I now live by this principle."

def•i•ni•tion

The Arabic word for destiny is **qadr**, which literally means to measure, while the Persian word for the same basic concept is *kismet*, which means a person's allotted fate. (Kismet is derived itself from the Arabic word **qisma,** which means division, fate, or allotment.)

The animals answered him, saying, "O wise one, don't be so cautious, for it will do you no good against fate. Relying upon caution is the very essence of trouble and calamity. Go now and put your trust in God, for trusting in God is far better. Don't fight against fate, O strong and fierce one, or fate might pick a fight with you. It's best to be compliant in the face of God's command; that way, no punishing blow will come from the Lord of the Dawn."

"You have a point," the lion replied, "but if merely trusting in God was the only guide, surely the Prophet's example must be useful, too. The Prophet declared for all to hear, 'Trust in God and then tie your camel.' Also, pay attention to the importance of the saying, 'The one who works is loved by God.' Don't use reliance upon God as a way to become neglectful of the means to gain success."

The animals answered him, saying, "Then consider the work offered by the weakest of God's creatures as a mouthful of false hope measured by the size of the appetite. There can be no better work than to trust in God. What can be more beloved to God than resigning one's self to His will? As long as a child is too weak to carry anything or run, he has nothing to ride on but the neck of his father. The One Who gives us rain from the sky can also, by His mercy, give us bread, as well."

"You have a point," the lion replied, "but the Lord of His servants has set a ladder before our feet. Gradually we must climb up toward the roof. To wait for what is needed is to get lost in foolish hopes. You have feet, so why do you act as if you were lame? You have hands, so why do you hide your fingers? When a master puts a shovel into the hands of his servant, he knows exactly what he has to do without a word being spoken. The hand and the shovel are both signs of God, and our power to think is our clear directive. When you pay attention to His signs then you'll devote your life to following what you've been directed to do. The exercise of free will is the method for thanking God for all His gifts. You're expectation of being taken care of is the denial of His gifts. If you want to trust in God, then trust Him through your work. Plant a seed and then rely upon the Great One."

Then all the animals began to argue with him, saying, "Yet, greedy ones have used work to attain their (unworthy) desires! So many other men and women who worked—why didn't they achieve success! They all failed in their plans and actions, while the plans and actions of the Creator remained."

This is an illustrated page from a fifteenth-century Persian manuscript of Kalila *and* Dimna.

"Yes," the lion replied, "but at the same time think about the efforts of the prophets and the faithful. God caused their striving to bear fruit, even though they suffered from oppression, heat, and cold. Everything they set out to do was good, for everything done by a good person is good. Their nets caught the bird of Heaven, and all their shortcomings became a means to improve."

The lion then continued to give many proofs like this, so much so that those who relied upon fate became tired of responding to him. The fox, deer, rabbit, and jackal abandoned arguing about fate and refrained from further discussion. Then they concluded their deal with the indignant lion, for they didn't want to risk losing the bargain they had offered. Thus, they all agreed that every day, the promised daily ration would come to the lion without fail, and that the lion would not ask for any more than that.

The Objection of the Rabbit

Every day, the animal who was chosen by a random drawing would run to the lion as fast as a cheetah (in order to be eaten by him). When this cup finally fell upon the rabbit, he cried out, "How long must we suffer from this injustice?"

The rest of the animals said, "For so long now we've been sacrificing our lives in faithful (observance of our bargain). Are you trying to drag down our reputation, you rebel! In order for the lion not to be angered, you should go to him now. Run fast!"

"My friends," the rabbit answered, "give me some time, so I can use my cunning to rescue us from this disaster. From my cunning your lives will be saved, and this will be a legacy passed on to your children, as well."

The animals objected, saying, "You foolish donkey! Listen to us. Don't venture beyond what a mere rabbit can accomplish. What are you saying—that you have a plan that those better than you have never thought of? You're just overconfident. Fate is calling to us, so how can you speak like this?"

The rabbit replied, "My friends. God gave me inspiration. A wise plan has come to the mind of a weakling. The knowledge that God taught to bees is not available to lions or donkeys. If a bee learns how to build its house out of a juicy treat, then God opened to it the door of that knowledge."

Rumi's References

In Muslim folklore, the bee is considered one of the symbols of wisdom. This is based on the following passage from the Qur'an. "Your Lord inspired the bee to build its nests in hillsides, on trees, and in the structures that people erect. He inspired it to eat of every flowering fruit, and to follow humbly the wide paths of its Lord. They produce from within their bodies a drink of varying shades that is a source of healing for humanity. In this is a sign for people who reflect."
—Qur'an 16:67–69

"O nimble rabbit," the animals exclaimed, "tell us your plan." However, the rabbit replied, "One shouldn't reveal every secret, for sometimes the even number comes up odd, and sometimes the reverse happens. If you speak to a mirror in your innocence, the mirror might suddenly become unclear to you. Never speak about three things in your life: when you plan to leave your house to travel, how much gold you have, and what religious doctrines you hold dear, for there are many enemies lying in wait to attack when they know about these three things. Even if you told only one or two other people the secret, every secret that goes beyond the original two who share it will be spread everywhere."

The Lion Meets His Fate

Then the rabbit waited for some time before going to the lion— the one who planned to tear his prey with his sharp claws. Now, because the rabbit had waited so long, the lion was scratching at the ground and roaring. He cried out, "Didn't I predict that the promise of those pathetic creatures would be in vain and remain unfulfilled? Their empty words have deceived me! After this, I'll never listen to the empty words of any other again. O heart of mine! Tear them to pieces, don't hold back; tear their skins, for they're shielded by nothing more than skin."

Meanwhile, the rabbit delayed as much as he dared, running over his crafty plan in his mind. After a long while, he took to the road so he could utter a few secret truths into the ear of the lion. The lion, fraught with hunger and panic, saw the rabbit in the distance. He ran toward his prey confidently with an air of fierce determination about him. When he came close to the threshold bordering his lair, the lion shouted, "You villain! I'm one who's ripped elephants apart! Who are you, you weak rabbit, that you should throw my summons down in the dust?"

"Have mercy!" cried the rabbit. "I have an excuse, if you'll permit me to explain. Consider the excuse of one who has suffered injustice. After breakfast, I set out to come here toward you with a friend of mine. The assembly of animals had chosen, for your sake, another rabbit to accompany me as my companion. On the road, another lion came and attacked us as we were on our way to you. I said to him, 'We are the slaves of the king of kings.' He replied, 'The king of kings! Who is that? He should be disgraced! Don't mention any low-born idiot in my presence. I'll tear both you and your king to shreds, if you and your friend try to escape.' Then I told him, 'Let me see my king one last time and tell him your message.' He then told me, 'Leave your friend here with me as my guarantee, and if you don't return, you'll be sacrificing his life to my law.' We begged and pleaded with him to no avail, for my friend was so much bigger and fatter than me. Now it appears that the road from the pasture to here is blocked by that new lion. So, give up all hope of ever getting any more allowance from us animals. I'm telling you the truth, even though the truth is bitter. If you want any more of us to come to you, then you must clear the way first."

"Come on then!" the lion exclaimed. "In God's name, lead the way. Let me see where he is, and if you're really telling the truth."

The rabbit then led the lion like a guide toward his trap, toward the deep well he had picked out to end his life. Thus, the pair traveled on until they reached the well, which the rabbit had deceitfully disguised under a pile of straw. When the lion came near to the well, he noticed that the rabbit slowed down and stepped back.

"Why have you stepped back?" the lion asked, "Let's keep moving."

"How can I take a step further," the rabbit asked, "when I have no feeling left in either hand or foot? My soul is shaking and my courage has fled."

"Out of all your misgivings," the lion said, "tell me why you're so afraid now."

"The lion I told you about lives in this hole." The rabbit explained. "While he's in there he's safe from any harm. All wise creatures choose to live in the bottom of a hole because solitude is the only way anyone can find peace."

"Now come on," the lion said, "my strike will knock him out. Go and see if that lion is in there now."

"I cannot move from fear of his ferocity." The rabbit cried. "Perhaps you will come along beside me, so that with your help I can open my eyes and look into the hole."

Footprints of the Master

Rumi's use of animal characters in his writing generally occurs only in the *Mathnawi*. His other books, such as the *Divan*, also use many metaphors, yet those allegories are usually drawn from the material world (celestial bodies, plants, etc.) or from philosophy, emotion, and literature.

When the lion took his place at the rabbit's side, they both began to run toward the disguised well. As soon as they looked down into it, the image of both the lion and the rabbit was reflected upon the water. The lion saw his own distorted reflection—with a plump rabbit standing to his side. When he saw what he thought was his enemy, the lion leapt straight down into the well and landed in the water. He fell into the well (of doom) that he had dug with his own sinfulness (and he drowned); his sins came back to haunt him.

Then the rabbit was overjoyed at his salvation and he ran back toward the animals until he passed over the long desert. He skipped elatedly all along the path back to the meadow, for he had seen the lion die in the well. He clapped his hands for joy, because he had escaped from the hand of death.

"Rejoice!" the rabbit cried as he returned. "The one who smashed many a head with his claws—well, the broom of death has swept him away like so much trash!"

Mathnawi I, condensed from lines 899–1389

The story ends with the rabbit explaining to the celebrating animals that they shouldn't get too happy, for the world had deceived them into believing that things just happened from divine providence. Yes, God helped the animals in this instance, but only because one of them took the initiative and became worthy of that help, as God willed. Indeed, the lesson of this story comes full circle. The animals had debated with the lion about fate versus free will. They were convinced that they must submit to whatever befell them, for if it happened to them, then it must be God's will. Although the lion tried his best to convince them that free will was a complement to fate and that fate, or destiny, was moved by the actions of people, still the animals were keen to merely submit to being eaten at regular intervals. The lion, who warned that he had an inner nature of his own he had to wrestle with, then happily agreed, for who would turn down a free meal from an insistent and willing dish!

The irony is that, while the lion came to rely on fate for his food, it was the willful action of one of the animals that undid him in the end. Thus, the rabbit, who learned the lessons of fate and free will on a deeper level, counseled his fellow animals to lift their heads and not rely only upon what appears to happen to them, but to take an active role in their lives. Then, after that, they can hold out hope for the best from God. This is wise counsel for our own lives, the realization that fate and free-will must each play their roles, like the yin and yang of Chinese philosophy. Too much reliance on one puts the other out of balance. Act as you are able in your life and never be complacent with your circumstances unless you've tried what you could to improve them. Then, when things are beyond your reasonable capacity, accept the results, for that is truly your fate.

The Lazy Dog

In this last selection, Rumi conveys the essential lesson that we must not become complacent in our lives. Here is what he wrote:

In the winter, the bones of a dog are drawn together; the biting frost makes him appear small. It was then that one dog said, "Because my body is so puny (from the effects of the cold), I must build a house of stone to stay warm. When summer next arrives, I'll build such a house to protect me from freezing."

When the summer finally arrived, his bones expanded in relief, and his coat grew sleek. When he saw himself so limber and sturdy, he said, "What house could ever hold me!" Then he grew even stronger (as the summer progressed), and eventually he retreated to a shady spot to rest; he was a lazy, well-fed, cowardly, and self-assured dog. His mind spoke to him, saying, "Build that house now, O uncle!" But his ego replied, "How can I stay in a mere house? Answer me that."

When you're stricken with pain and your greedy bones shrink down and lose their expansive reach, you cry out in repentance, "I'll build that house of shelter and be safe from the harsh winter." Yet, when the pain is gone and your greed has grown stronger, your desire to build a safe place of refuge leaves you, just as it did that dog.

Mathnawi III, 2885–2894

This is a recurring theme in Rumi's writing: when times are good, we forget what's in our best interests and become overconfident, but when times are hard, our dilemma becomes crystal clear and we vow that we'll reform ourselves, if only we had a second chance. However, when we've grown strong and capable once more, we forget all about what we suffered. We discard the lessons, the realizations, and then we go on just as heedless as we were before. This is the bitter cycle that a far-sighted person seeks release from, which enables enlightenment to take root. Alternating periods of certainty and fear play havoc with our inner selves, making us ripe for a very hard landing when all our options have expired, unless we take a new approach.

Wisdom of the Ages

Rumi wrote in his *Divan*: "You do wrong and hope to get back good, though wrong deserves only wrong in return. God is merciful and kind, but even so, if you plant barley, wheat won't grow."

Balance is the key. When a person gains a sense of balance and no longer exults too much from success or laments too much from failure, then she can look at the world more deliberately and protect herself from the roller coaster of hope and fear. For the balanced person, her sense of safety or well-being is no longer tied to the ups and downs of life. When the years are good, it's a time to be cautious, thankful, and humble; when times are tough, lessons must be learned, vows must be more modest in scope, and despair must be mitigated by more motivation to get out of the slump.

In the end, for balanced people, life no longer has the power to alter our self-perception, for we become the masters of perception, even as we realize that we are no longer trapped in our dealings with the world. Rumi beckons us to escape the cycle and abandon exultant overconfidence and abject despair. Life happens regardless of what we want, and the wisdom is not to let it control how we feel, and realizing we're just an unpaid actor on this stage set by someone else.

The Least You Need to Know

- For Rumi, destiny or fate is one part free will with one part allowance for the unforeseen acts of God.

- Life is a place filled with distractions; learn to ignore them and get on with your affairs.

- It is better to maintain a balanced sense of self in good times and in bad, rather than to be boastful in success and hopeless in hardship.

- The farsighted person escapes the traps of life by recognizing them and departing from the environment in which he or she is set.

Chapter 12

Stories of the Seeker

In This Chapter

◆ Learning how Rumi used allegorical stories to impart his main body of thought and philosophy

◆ Discovering some of Rumi's most memorable tales of insight and wisdom

◆ Exploring how Rumi wove historical figures into his narratives with surprising results

◆ Understanding the differences between the various literary styles that Rumi employed

One of the main techniques Rumi used to impart wisdom was that of the "teaching story." Modern scientists have already demonstrated that the human brain appears to be wired to respond to and learn from narratives, and thus it's no wonder that every religion and even every secular body of knowledge employs stories of some kind to focus the reader's attention. (Have you ever wondered why there were so many story problems in math class?) For his part, Rumi's entire *Mathnawi* is like one large extended story, punctuated by nuggets of wisdom and commentary. In contrast, his *Divan* is more ecstatic and abstract in tone. Is it any wonder then that the *Mathnawi* has had wider appeal through the centuries over the more enigmatic and personalized *Divan*?

Rumi literally mined the literary world of his day for characters to populate his tales. He also drew liberally upon historic personalities and events. And, of course, he employed countless allusions to verses from the Qur'an and events from the life of Prophet Muhammad and the notables of his time. All of these elements and more are woven together seamlessly in the *Mathnawi*. In this chapter, we present some of Rumi's more memorable and poignant teaching stories. Given that many of them in their original form span dozens of pages, often with frequent digressions, these are condensed versions of the choicest of them with the main storylines in tact.

The Linguist and the Sailor

> A linguist who thought very highly of himself took passage on a ship one day. While on the open sea he turned to a sailor and asked, "Have you ever studied languages?"
>
> The sailor replied, "No." Thereupon the linguist chided him, saying, "Then you've missed out on half your life!" The sailor felt humiliated, and he spoke no more after that.
>
> Soon a fierce wind arose on the sea and the boat lurched toward a raging whirlpool. The sailor shouted to the linguist, "Do you know how to swim?"
>
> "No, my well-spoken and good man," the terrified linguist called back to him.
>
> "Then, my dear linguist," the sailor replied, "you've lost your entire life, for this boat is about to sink in that whirlpool."
>
> *Mathnawi* I, 2835–2840

We human beings often delve deep into specialized fields in the course of our careers. There's nothing wrong with that, and experience makes the best kind of resource when that particular skill is called upon. There is a hidden danger in academic or career success, however, and that is in the possibility of specialization prejudice. In the same way that people can judge others by their race, class, or appearance, there can also be a kind of snobbery connected with one's profession. A person who is oriented only toward material success and achievement may consider his expertise to be some sort of mark of nobility or uniqueness. Perhaps he may begin to feel that his own area of knowledge is more important than other areas of knowledge.

One of the greatest lessons of living in a diverse society is the realization that we all need each other, given that we all bring a different type of essential skill to the table. This is a part of being thoughtful and balanced. While it is assumed that an auto mechanic might not make the best surgeon, how many doctors cannot fix their own cars? While a seamstress may have trouble with managing an international conglomerate, how many executives cannot sew their own clothes? Arrogance of profession has no place in the world of human interaction. We are all experts in our own field of knowledge—or on our way to becoming so—and one day the knowledge we may look down upon may be the very thing that will save our life later on.

The King and the Band of Thieves

The following story takes place during the reign of Sultan Mahmoud of Ghazni (d. 1030). Following the practice established from the earliest days of the caliphs of Islam, Sultan Mahmoud would sometimes walk the streets of his capital city (in what is now Afghanistan) in disguise to check on the welfare of his citizens. Rumi begins the story thusly:

> King Mahmoud was wandering in the city alone one night when he came upon a band of thieves. When they saw him they asked, "Who are you, good sir?"

> "I am one of you," answered the king. Thereupon one of the thieves proposed to his fellows, "O gathered band of experts in the devious arts, let each of us describe his own unique talent. Let him describe to the rest of us what special skill he may possess in this late-night meeting."

Rumi's References _____

Sultan Mahmoud of Ghazni (who ruled in present-day Afghanistan, Iran, and northern India) was a favorite subject of mystic writers (Rumi included) due to his seemingly ethereal attachment to his attendant, Ayaz, with all the implications of selfless friendship and union it implied. In fact, the relationship between the two men became something of a staple in Sufi literature for depicting the model of an ideal beloved and his mirror-soul.

One of the thieves said, "O you men who would reveal your talents, my special skill lies between my two ears, for I know what a dog is saying when it barks." The rest of the group said, "That's not worth much at all!"

Another thief said, "O you men who worship gold, my skill is contained entirely in my eyesight. If I see someone at night, I can instantly recognize him in the day without any doubt."

Another one said, "My skill is in my arm, for I can dig tunnels with the strength of my own hands."

Another one said, "My skill is in my nose, for I can tell the difference between different kinds of soils. I've come to know the secret of the prophetic saying, 'Men are like goldmines,' for when I smell the soil of the earth, I know how much gold it hides and what kind of mine it is. One mine may have a fortune in gold, while another may not be worth the effort to dig into it."

The last one said, "Now see here, my skill lies in my grip, for I can throw a lasso as high as a mountain."

Then the gathered thieves turned to the (disguised) king and said, "O man of ability, what is your special skill or talent?"

The king answered them, saying, "My special talent lies in my beard, for I can release criminals from punishment. When criminals are being handed over to the executioners, as soon as I move my beard, they're saved! When I move my beard in mercy, the executioners cease all their slaying and torture."

The band of thieves exclaimed, "You're our leader, then, for one day you may be the cause of our salvation on a sore day." (Then they all set out together to rob the palace of the king.)

(When they came near the palace,) suddenly, a dog barked to the right, and the first of them said, "That dog is saying, 'The Sultan is with you.'" Then one of them leaned down to smell the ground on a hill (near the palace wall). He said, "This plot belongs to the house of a widow."

Sultan Mahmoud of Ghazni is shown in this Persian painting shaking hands with an old Shaykh. —Tehran Museum of Contemporary Art.

Then the skillful lasso-thrower threw his rope over the wall (of the palace) and by this means, all of them got over the high wall. When the thief whose skill was scent smelled the ground again, he said, "Under this soil lies the treasury of a high king."

The digger dug a tunnel and broke into the treasure room; each of the thieves carried off something from the treasury. In fact, the band made away with a large amount of gold, gold-embroidered cloth, and even huge pearls. They quickly hid their loot.

Unbeknownst to them, however, the king made note of their hide-out, their identities, their physical appearances, and their homes. Then he slipped away from them and went back to the palace. The next morning he told his officials all about his adventure, causing determined officers to set out in hot pursuit of the thieves.

Soon the thieves were shackled together and brought into the audience chamber of the king. They stood there in fear for their lives. Thus, they were assembled before the king's throne—and so it was that this moon of a king was their companion the night before!

The thief who had the power to recognize by day anyone whom he had seen at night saw the king on his throne and exclaimed, "This man was out and about with us last night as our comrade! This is the one who had a special skill in his beard—we've been apprehended on account of his inquiries!"

Then that thief, whose eye recognized the king, opened his mouth to address his fellows, saying, "This king was with you, and he saw all our actions and heard all our words in secret. I will beg forgiveness for all of you from him, for he cannot turn away from the one who recognizes him."

def•i•ni•tion

The Arabic term **sultan** means a ruler or king. This term came into vogue among the increasingly powerful Turkic tribes that gradually took command of much of the central Muslim world, all but supplanting the previous term for leader, which was **caliph**.

Then he addressed the king, saying, "O king, whose plans are hidden, the time has come for you to graciously make a sign with your beard to forgive. Each of us has revealed his special talent, and the exercise of each has done nothing but brought us bad luck—all save for the talent of the one whose excellent sight recognized the Sultan from the darkness of the night. Those skills have caused our necks to be bound, and from those special talents we've been waylaid and brought down." On this day, the king was too ashamed not to grant the request of the one who recognized the king at night.

Listen, you must never look down upon those who have no concern for their reputation, for you must look to what they have inside (their hearts). How many fine pieces of gold have been tarnished with soot to make them appear as iron in order to save them from being taken in plunder?

Condensed from *Mathnawi* VI, 2816–2921

In this story, the king is actually a metaphor for God, and the thieves, with all their skills, are we human beings. Despite our schemes and plans, God is in our midst and knows all the secrets of our hearts. When we are brought for judgment, the one among us who clearly recognizes the king may be the cause for clemency for so many of the rest of us, even though we would otherwise deserve to be punished for all the wrong that we did. Even as God will look to our inner worth, we, too, must learn to value others among us for more than our outward accomplishments or perceived talents. Most important of all, those who seem unconcerned about material success and fame—they may be the ones whose intercession may profit us the most.

The Man Who Befriended a Bear

A dragon was pulling a bear into its jaws; a brave man arrived and rescued it. Brave men are a source of aid in this world and react whenever the cry of the oppressed reaches them. They listen for the cry of the oppressed from every direction, and instantly run there to help, just like the mercy of God!

In the same way, when the bear had cried out for help against the dragon, that brave man rescued it from the fight. Cunning and courage helped each other that day, and through this union of strength, the man killed the dragon.

After it had been saved from the dragon, the bear realized it had received an act of kindness from that brave man. Like the dog who dwelt with the Sleepers of the Cave, that poor bear began to follow after the one who saved it from its travail.

Rumi's References

Chapter 18 of the Qur'an contains a summarized version of the Christian legend of the Sleepers of the Cave. According to this story, some Christian youths escaped persecution in Roman times by going into a sort of hibernation in a cave. They emerged many years later when persecution was no more. Their faithful dog Qitmir remained at their side, guarding the entrance to the cave.

That man of faith, being exhausted, laid his head down to rest, whereupon the bear devotedly took up watch over him. Soon a certain man passed by and said to the brave man (in astonishment), "What's going on here? My brother, why is this bear so attached to you?"

Then the first man told the newcomer all about his adventure and of his struggle with the dragon. After he had finished telling the tale, however, the visitor warned, "You fool, don't get too attached to a bear. A fool's friendship is worse than his hatred. You should drive this bear away by any means you can."

However, the first man thought to himself, "By God! He's only saying that because he's jealous." Then he told the visitor, "Why do you only see the danger in this bear? Look at how much he loves me!"

The visitor answered him, saying, "The love of fools is a delusion. My jealousy is better than this bear's affection. Come on now; let's drive this bear away together. Don't choose a bear for a friend over one of your own kind."

"Go away," the first man said, "and mind your own business, you jealous man." Then the visitor implored him further, saying, "This is my business, and this bear is not part of the bounty you were to receive. I'm not worth less than this bear, noble sir. Leave it so I can be your friend. I'm worried sick for you. Don't go into the forest with a bear like this."

Even though the visitor said all of these things, the first man seemingly heard none of it. Suspicion is a thick barrier in the heart of a man. "I'm tired," the first man said, "Go away and leave me alone."

(After the visitor left,) the man fell asleep. Soon the bear diligently began to drive away the insects that were buzzing all around the sleeping man, but to no avail. Several times, it swished them away from the young man's face, but they would rush back and land on him once more.

The bear became angry at the flies and then it stormed off. It picked up a big rock from the cliff side. When it returned, it saw the flies sitting comfortably on the face of the sleeper. The bear then took up that big rock and struck at the flies to make them leave once and for all.

The stone wound up crushing the sleeping man's face to dust, and thus gave rise to the well-known proverb, "The love of a fool is like the love of a bear: his love is hate and his hate is love."

Condensed from *Mathnawi* II, 1932–2140

When a person draws someone close to herself out of love, she must beware of the potential danger such affection may unwittingly unleash. How many are the people who have seen the light of love in others, without recognizing the danger they are capable of, even if they don't intend any harm?

Where Is Your Camel?

During the fabled days of medieval Baghdad, many stories were told of wandering holy men and women who fearlessly taught wisdom to the kings of the realm. One such holy man was the erudite scholar, Ibrahim ibn Adham (d. 777), of whom Rumi wrote extensively in the *Mathnawi*. (Ibn Adham was dear to Sufis, having given up a kingdom in Balkh to become a wandering Sufi mystic.) In this vignette, Ibn Adham was staying in the opulent palace of the caliph, Abu Ja'far al-Mansur (d. 775), and he found an ingenious way to bring home to the king the point that material wealth opens no doorways to heaven. Here's what Rumi recounts:

As he rested upon his throne, the king, who was a man of good reputation, noticed the sounds of tramping feet and loud cries coming from the roof. When he heard that loud commotion on the roof of the palace, he said to himself, "Who dares to do this?"

He leaned out of the palace window and shouted upward, saying, "Who's there? If it's not a man, perhaps it's a genie!" An astonishing group of people (led by a Shaykh) lowered their heads down from the roof and said, "We're out here tonight looking for something!"

"Huh?" (The caliph replied). "What are you looking for up there?" "We're looking for camels," they answered. Thereupon (the caliph scolded them), saying, "Listen you! Whoever thought to search for camels on a roof?"

Then they called back down to him in answer, asking, "Whoever thought to find God while seated on a throne?"

Mathnawi IV, 829–834

The Hero of Qazwin

In this story, set in the Persian town of Qazwin, we learn of how one man's courage was put to the test in a way he didn't expect. Rumi begins the action in this way:

"Listen to this tale from the storyteller, and what it says of the ways of the people of Qazwin. They tattoo themselves with blue ink delivered lightly on the point of a needle on their bodies, hands, and shoulders, taking every care not to feel any pain.

A certain warrior of Qazwin went to a tattoo artist and said to him, "Tattoo me in a more splendid way than usual."

"O Brave one," said the artist, "what figure would you have me imprint?" The man answered him, saying, "Prick in the figure of a raging lion, for Leo is my sign. Yes, tattoo a lion. Go all out and inject plenty of blue ink."

"Where would you like me to place the tattoo?" asked the artist. "Prick the gorgeous idol on my shoulder," the man replied boldly. However, as soon as the artist began to stick his needle in, the pain erupted in the man's shoulder. The hero began groaning and said, "O noble one, you're killing me. What shape are you tattooing?"

"You asked me to do a lion," the artist replied. "Then what part of the lion did you start with?" the man asked. "I started on the tail," he answered.

"My close comrade," he cried, "leave off the tail. I nearly lost my breath from this lion's tail and rump; it was like his rump choked off my windpipe! Let the lion have no tail, O maker of lions, for my heart is faint from the pricking of the needle."

Then the artist began to prick on another part of the man's shoulder fearlessly, without any concern or kindness. Thereupon the man cried out once more in pain, "Which part of the lion is that?"

The artist replied, "That's his ear, my good man." "O Doctor," he moaned, "let him have no ears then. Forget the ears and make his mane short."

Then the artist began working on another part, yet once again the man of Qazwin let out a scream, saying, "What part are you working on now in this third spot?" The artist answered wearily, saying, "That's the lion's belly, good sir." "Then let the lion have no belly!" he cried. "It hurts too much; don't prick on me any more!"

Wisdom of the Ages

Rumi wrote of the necessity of pain in the process of unlocking the soul in these words from his *Divan*: "If you have the strength, don't wear the robe of love, but if you do, don't moan about catastrophe. The robe will disappear in a fire, but bear the pain in silence. What's poison now is merely the juice of life in the hereafter."

The artist became flustered and froze in confusion. He remained there standing for some time with his fingers in his teeth. Suddenly, the master threw his needle to the ground and said, "Has this ever happened to anyone else in the whole world? Whoever heard of a lion without a tail or a head or a belly? Even God never created a lion like this. My brother, endure the pain of the blade so you can be liberated from your (fearful) lower self. The sky and the moon bow down in adoration to those who have escaped from their own sense of existence. Whoever has extinguished his lower self will find the sun and the clouds at his command. Since his heart has learned how to light the candle (of truth), the sun can no longer harm him."

Mathnawi I, 2981–3005

The hero of Qazwin was able to endure every pain of battle, yet when he had to endure a pinprick, he was faint with fear. How many of us are aware of our own weaknesses, even though we appear invulnerable in all respects? Perhaps when we're wounded from an unexpected direction, it's an opportunity for us to examine the real depth of our convictions and strengths. Rumi counsels us to accept the pain and to purify the hidden defects that we wouldn't have otherwise known about. Then, our value will be complete, the pain of the material world will no longer be so vexing, and we'll have a clearer path toward the way of truth.

The Man Who Fled from Death

One day a nobleman burst into King Solomon's hall of justice. He was pale with despair and his lips were blue with fright. "O noble sir," Solomon asked, "what's wrong with you?" The man answered him, saying, "The Angel of Death came and looked at me with eyes filled with anger and hate."

The king then said, "Come now, what favor would you ask of me?" The nobleman replied, saying, "O protector of my life, order the wind to bear me swiftly (on a ship) to India, for maybe when your servant has arrived there it will save his life."

> **Footprints of the Master**
>
> The name of the Angel of Death in Islamic theology is Azra'il. He is in charge of taking the souls of those who are destined to die according to a schedule set by God.

Therefore, Solomon ordered the wind to bear the nobleman swiftly over the sea to the farthest part of India. On the next day, however, when it was time for Solomon to meet the Angel of Death, he asked him, "Did you look on that faithful man of mine with anger—to force him into exile far from his home?"

The Angel of Death replied, "When did I look at him in anger? When I saw him passing by, I looked at him in astonishment, for God had commanded me, saying, 'Listen! Take his soul while he's in India.' In bewilderment, I said to myself, 'Even if he had 100 wings, it would be a far journey for him to make—all the way to India!'"

This is how you must consider all your affairs in this world. Open your eyes and see! Whom should we run from? From ourselves? Oh, how foolish! Whom should we take from? From God? Oh, the crime!

Condensed from *Mathnawi* I, 956–970

This is a variation of a very famous and well-known story in classical Muslim civilization. Its roots go back to a saying of Muhammad in which he declared, "No one can know what he will earn tomorrow, even as no one can know in which land he will die." In this version of the classic Solomon story that illustrates this principle, the foolish man thinks he can outrun Death, only to wind up in the place where Death was supposed to take his life—a miracle for which even Death was amazed.

The moral of this tale is simply that people must realize they have little control over their ultimate end. When this is truly accepted internally, then one layer of fear and uncertainty can be removed. No one knows what we will earn tomorrow, and no amount of planning or precaution will preserve our lives if it's our time to go. On the other hand, if it's not our time, no amount of destruction or danger will affect us in the least. Thus, the best way to live life is not to get too comfortable with it. Strive to live a life in preparation for leaving it, and then material concerns will have that much less of a hold upon us. This is one more piece of the puzzle in learning to be more at ease with one's ultimate fate.

Don't Deal in "If"

There once was a newcomer to town; he desperately searched for a house to dwell within. A friend of his took him to see an old dilapidated building. Then he said to the newcomer, "If only this house had a roof, then it could be a home for you close to my own. Your family could also live quite comfortably here, as well—if only it had an extra room."

The newcomer looked at his companion and said, "Yes, it would be nice to live near friends, no doubt about that, but my dear friend, you cannot live in 'if.'"

Mathnawi II, 739–742

It's nice to hope for well and good, yet at some point "what ifs" have to give way to concrete realities. A goal is only a dream until hard work actually makes it happen. Nothing ever came to a dreamer without him at least holding out his hand to receive it. This is the least amount of effort one can do. A life jacket may be thrown to you in the churning ocean of life, yet how many never do more than look at the possibilities that the life jacket represents—and then drown in their own fantasies? Direct your attention at what will keep you afloat, yet also make an effort to take a hold of it, and then start to swim toward the shore! The seeker finds because he's willing to go out on the road. Rumi shows us that nobody ever succeeded in this world by relying only on "if."

The Least You Need to Know

- We all have different talents and one is not more valuable than the other, except when that particular talent is needed the most. When such a time of need has passed, it becomes equal with the rest once more.

- Sufis generally hold that material wealth and acquisition are actually impediments to getting in touch with the inner spirit. The inner senses are dulled when physical desires get more attention than them.

- The time and place of our death is fixed, and therefore we need not fret about it in uncertainty. It is better to live a life in preparation for one's exit.

- We all have a responsibility to work for what we desire. Life cannot thrive merely on dreams and hopes.

A

A Timeline of Rumi's Life

Rumi led a colorful life filled with fascinating experiences, characters, and travels. He was born in 1207 in the city of Balkh, in what we call Afghanistan today. He passed away in 1273 in the city of Konya, present-day Turkey, after a life of both spiritual and physical adventure. Below is a brief sketch of the major events of his life.

1152

Rumi's father, Baha'uddin Walad, is born in the district of Balkh, a province of Persia (now in modern-day Afghanistan).

1207 (September 30)

Jalaluddin Muhammad (Rumi) is born in the town of Wakhsh, an outlying district of greater Balkh (about 155 miles to the north in present-day Tajikistan). This is the city where his father was employed as a teacher.

1212

Rumi's father, Baha'uddin Walad, takes his family to live in Samarkand (in present-day Uzbekistan) to escape the ravages of a regional ruler (and warlord) entitled Ala'uddin Khwarizm Shah.

1219–1222

Due to the imminent threat of Mongol invasion, Rumi's father then takes his family out of Central Asia and they make a pilgrimage to Mecca. Along the way, they stop in Nishapur where Rumi has the chance to meet with Fariduddin 'Attar, one of Islam's most celebrated mystics. They also enter Baghdad for a short time. Baha'uddin gives Rumi a classical Islamic education during his formative years and a book of his mystical thoughts called the *Ma'arif.*

1222

Rumi's mother, Mu'minah Khatun, passes away.

1224 or 1226

Rumi is married to Ghevher (Jawhar) Khatun, the daughter of Lala Sharafuddin of Samarkand.

1226 or 1227

Rumi's first child, Sultan Walad, is born. Rumi's brother, Ala'uddin, passes away.

1228

Baha'uddin brings his family to dwell in the small town of Iconium in Konya (present-day Turkey), at the invitation of a local prince of the Seljuk Turks. He takes up the job of a religious teacher at a new academy. Rumi's second child is born, whom he names Ala'uddin in honor of his deceased brother.

1231

Rumi's father passes away in Konya in the spring. Rumi is appointed by the Sultan to be the head of his departed father's academy.

1232

Burhanuddin Muhaqqiq, a disciple of Rumi's father, arrives in Konya and reveals to Rumi that his father was a secret spiritual master. Rumi, who had been an unassuming Muslim lawyer and preacher, begins to ponder this new revelation.

1232–1236

Burhanuddin becomes Rumi's teacher and he sends Rumi to Syria to continue his religious studies. He may have heard the speeches of Ibn 'Arabi there, who was the greatest scholar of the day and a prominent mystic. Rumi composes some couplets in Arabic.

1237

Rumi returns to Konya with an impressive education at his disposal. He takes over the leadership of the many students that Burhanuddin managed in his father's old academy. Rumi is also a frequent preacher during Friday prayers in the mosque, a tradition he continues off and on for the rest of his life.

1240

Burhanuddin leaves Konya and passes away some time later in the nearby town of Kayseri. By this time, Rumi is beginning to explore the spiritual dimensions of Islam on a deeper level. His poetic compositions increase in number.

1242–1243

Rumi's wife, Ghevher (Jawhar) passes away.

1244 (October)

Rumi meets Shamsuddin of Tabriz for the first time by chance in a market. He becomes inseparable from this enigmatic stranger and forsakes most contact with his family and students. Shamsuddin, sensing the ill will his presence is causing among Rumi's family, students, and reputation, suddenly disappears about three months later.

1246 (circa)

Shamsuddin is discovered in Damascus, Syria. Rumi sends his son to escort him back to Konya. Shamsuddin then visits with Rumi, who cannot bear to be parted from him again. Rumi arranges for Shamsuddin to marry a woman from his extended household and then he spends most of his time in deep conversation with his dear friend, who discusses arcane spiritual topics with him. Rumi's students grow jealous once more.

1248

Shamsuddin disappears under mysterious circumstances. (Ala'uddin, the son of Rumi, is suspected as the ringleader in Shamsuddin's murder, though this is never proven.) Rumi is heartbroken and becomes more philosophical and introspective. He begins to compose an ever-greater number of poems dedicated to the memory of Shamsuddin, which he calls the *Collection of Shams*, or *Diwan-i Shams*, also known as the *Divan*.

1249–1250

Rumi meets a disciple of his old master Burhanuddin, a goldsmith named Salahuddin Faridun Zarkub, who becomes Rumi's new mentor. Rumi spends much time in his company, leading his students to again become jealous. This time, Rumi is more compromising in the amount of time he spends with his new mentor, as opposed to the inordinate amount of time he spent with Shamsuddin before.

1251

The local Seljuk ruler is replaced by a trio of puppet rulers under Mongol influence. Rumi comments upon this in some of his letters.

1250–1255

Rumi marries a Christian convert to Islam, Kira Khatun. She bears him three children: two boys and a girl. Rumi attracts an ever-growing number of students to his spiritual teachings and poetry. Even non-Muslims begin to attend his lectures.

1256

The former vizier of Sultan Kayqubad becomes the ruler of the Seljuk state (under Mongol blessing) within which Rumi resides. He honors Rumi and supports his work for the rest of his life.

1258

Salahuddin Faridun Zarkub passes away. Rumi appoints Husamuddin Chelebi, his chief student, to lead his father's old academy. On a regional note, Baghdad, the capital of the 'Abbasid Caliphate, falls to the Mongols, sending shock waves through the Muslim world.

1259–1260 (circa)

Rumi begins work on his monumental book of poetry, the *Mathnawi*, at the behest of Husamuddin. Husamuddin records in writing the dictation of Rumi for the next several years. Rumi also writes many letters to friends and local government officials. A large number of these letters have survived to today.

1260

The Mongols are defeated in nearby Syria at the Battle of 'Ayn Jalut. The Mongol threat gradually recedes and the core of the Islamic world remains safe.

1262

Rumi begins work on the second volume of the *Mathnawi*. Rumi's son, Ala'uddin, passes away, and Rumi does not attend the funeral due to the suspicion that Ala'uddin was involved in Shamsuddin's disappearance. The writing of the *Mathnawi* is paused for a time due to the death of Husamuddin's wife.

1264

Work resumes on the *Mathnawi*.

1267

The *Mathnawi* is finalized and complete. It comprises six full volumes, consisting of about 25,600 couplets.

1273 (December 17)

Rumi falls ill. Physicians of all faiths try to remedy him, yet Rumi cheerfully seems resigned to death. Rumi finally passes away in Konya. His funeral is attended by multitudes of Christians, Jews, and Muslims. Rumi's disciple Husamuddin becomes the leader of Rumi's followers.

1284

Husamuddin dies and Rumi's eldest son, Sultan Walad, assumes the mantle of leadership.

1285–1312

Sultan Walad organizes the first rules for the ritual meditative dance known as the *sama'*. He also organizes Rumi's followers into a structured Sufi order known as the Mevlevi Order. He leads it until his death in 1312. The members of this group also record a book of Rumi's teachings, which they received from him, and entitle the work, *What Is in This Is in That*, or *Fihi Ma Fihi*. Seven of Rumi's sermons are also preserved, as well as the *Divan* and about 150 personal letters.

Appendix B

Rumi Resources

Popular collections in English of Rumi's work are a relatively recent phenomenon. Obviously, some collections are more representative of Rumi's genius than others, and some are more faithful to the meaning and intent of the original Persian text. Below is an abbreviated list of some of the more important translations of Rumi poetry in English.

Translations and Renderings of Rumi's Poetry

The Mathnawi of Jalaluddin Rumi, trans. by Reynold A. Nicholson

Signs of the Unseen: The Discourses of Jalaluddin Rumi, trans. by W. M. Thackston, Jr.

Discourses of Rumi, trans. by A. J. Arberry

Jewels of Remembrance, rendered by Camille and Kabir Helminski

The Essential Rumi, rendered by Coleman Barks et al.

The Soul of Rumi: A New Collection of Ecstatic Poems, rendered by Coleman Barks

Rumi: The Book of Love: Poems of Ecstasy and Longing, rendered by Coleman Barks

A Rumi Anthology, trans. by Reynold A. Nicholson

Rumi: Gardens of the Beloved, trans. by Maryam Mafi and Azima Melita Kolin

Selected Poems of the Divan-e Shams-e Tabrizi, trans. by Reynold A. Nicholson

Rumi and Islam: Selections from His Stories, Poems, and Discourses, rendered by Ibrahim Gamard

The Hundred Tales of Wisdom, trans. by Idris Shah

A Year with Rumi, rendered by Coleman Barks

Hush, Don't Say Anything to God: Passionate Poems of Rumi, translated by Shahram Shiva

Rumi: The Masnavi: Book One, trans. by Jawid Mojaddedi

The Rumi Collection, rendered by Kabir Helminski et al.

Biographies of Rumi

Rumi's World: The Life and Work of the Great Sufi Poet, by Annemarie Schimmel

A Moth to a Flame: The Story of the Great Sufi Poet Rumi, by Connie Zweig

The Life and Work of Jalaluddin Rumi, by Afzal Iqbal

Major Books That Influenced Rumi's Thought

The Meaning of the Holy Qur'an in Today's English, trans. by Yahiya Emerick

The Conference of the Birds, by Fariduddin 'Attar. Trans. by Afkham Darbandi and Dick Davis

The Drowned Book: Ecstatic and Earthly Reflections of Bahauddin the Father of Rumi, rendered by Coleman Barks and John Moyne

The Remembrance of Death and the Afterlife, by Abu Hamid Muhammad al-Ghazali. Trans. by T. J. Winter.

Asrar Nama (The Book of Secrets), by Fariduddin 'Attar

The Island of Animals, by the Brethren of Purity. Trans. by Denys Johnson-Davies

Muslim Saints and Mystics: Episodes from the Tadhkirat al-Auliya, by Fariduddin 'Attar. Trans. by A. J. Arberry.

The Story of Layla and Majnun, by Nizami Ganjavi. Trans. by Omega Publications

The Walled Garden of Truth: The Hadiqa, by Hakim Sanai. Trans. by David Pendlebury

Ibn-Al-Arabi: The Bezels of Wisdom, by Muhyuddin ibn 'Arabi. Trans. by R. W. J. Austin and Titus Burkhardt

Divine Sayings: The Mishkat Al-Anwar of Ibn 'Arabi, by Muhyuddin ibn 'Arabi. Trans. by Stephen Hertenstein

The Poems of Al-Mutanabbi, trans. by A. J. Arberry

Books Related to Rumi Studies

Teachings of Rumi, by Andrew Harvey

Me and Rumi: The Autobiography of Shams–I Tabrizi, trans. by Annemarie Schimmel and William Chittick

Jalal-Al-Din Al-Rumi: A Muslim Saint, Mystic, and Poet, by Emine Yeniterzi

Fundamentals of Rumi's Thought: A Mevlevi Sufi Perspective, by Sefik Can and M. Fethullah Gulen.

Rumi and the Whirling Dervishes, by Shems Freidlander and Annemarie Schimmel

The Gift: Poems by Hafiz, trans. by Daniel Ladinsky

Women Called to the Path of Rumi: The Way of the Whirling Dervish, by Shakina Reinhertz

The Sufi Path of Love: The Spiritual Teaching of Rumi, by William Chittick

Muhammad, by Yahiya Emerick

The Metaphysics of Rumi: A Critical and Historical Sketch, by Khalifa Abdul Hakim

'Attar and the Persian Sufi Tradition: The Art of Spiritual Flight, by Leonard Lewisohn

A Millennium of Classical Persian Poetry: A Guide to the Reading and Understanding of Persian Poetry from the Tenth to the Twentieth Century, by Wheeler M. Thackston

Audio/Visual Resources

Rumi: Poet of the Heart. Magnolia Films, DVD 2004

Reading Rumi in an Uncertain World. (Read by Robert Bly and Naomi Shihab Nye) Texas Nafas, DVD 2005

Rumi: The Wings of Love. (Read by Peter Boyle) Parabola Books, VHS 2002

Rumi: Voice of Longing. (Read by Coleman Barks) Sounds True, Audio CD 2003

I Want Burning. (Read by Coleman Barks) Sounds True, Audio CD 2001

Rumi. (Read by Coleman Barks) CBC Audio, Audio CD 2005

A Gift of Love: Deepak and Friends Present Music Inspired by the Love Poems of Rumi. Rasa Music, Audio CD 1998

Vision II: The Spirit of Rumi. (By Graeme Revell) Angel, Audio CD 1997

When Days Have No Nights. (Rumi poems set to music by Mischa Rutenberg) MorPrem, Audio CD 2000.

Rumi Poetry. (Read by Christopher Love) World Sangha Publishing, Audio CD 2005

Through Eternity: Homage to Molavi (Rumi). (Live music by the Dastan Ensemble) Sounds True Direct, Audio CD 1999

Mevlana: Music of the Whirling Dervishes. (Music by Nezih Uzel) Blue Note Records, Audio CD 1997

Breeze at Dawn: The Poems of Rumi in Song. (Music and Rumi poems read by Dale Zola) Mahata, Audio CD 1999

Say I Am You. (Rumi poems read by W. A. Mathieu) Cold Mountain Music, Audio CD 2003

Lament of the Reed. (Rumi poems read aloud) Musicrama/Koch, Audio CD 2001

Organizations

Mevlana Celaluddin Rumi
www.mevlana.net

This is the official website of the Mevlevi Order under the direction of direct descendants of Rumi.

Mevlevi Order of America
www.hayatidede.org
E-mail: info@hayatidede.org

This is an American branch of the international order. It has multiple branches all over North America.

Dervish Retreat Center
www.whirlingdervish.org
E-mail: khadija@whirlingdervish.org
Phone: 607-272-0694

This is the site for a retreat for the teaching of whirling as practiced by the Mevlevi dervish order located in Spencer, NY.

The Threshold Society
www.sufism.org
E-mail: mevlana@cruzio.com
Phone: 831-685-3995

This is another American branch of the international Mevlevi Order. It has links to several other chapters across the country.

Sarihan Exhibition and Cultural Center
www.sarihan1249.com
E-mail: info@sarihan1249.com

A Mevlevi organization in Turkey.

The Foundation of Universal Lovers of Jalaluddin Rumi
www.emav.org
E-mail: info@emav.org

A Mevlevi organization in Turkey.

Websites

There are literally thousands of websites on the life and work of Rumi. I've selected for you some of the best and most representative of the broad range of offerings available to discover.

www.sufism.org

www.dar-al-masnavi.org

www.rumirecordsshop.com

www.mevlana.net

www.rumiforum.org

www.semazen.net

www.poetry-chaikhana.com/R/RumiJelaludd/index.htm

www.rumi.org.uk (or) www.khamush.com

www.rumionfire.com

groups.yahoo.com/group/Ruminations

groups.yahoo.com/group/Sunlight

www.sln.org.uk/re/whirling.htm

www.geocities.com/SoHo/Studios/9594/mevlana.htm

godlas.myweb.uga.edu/rumimevlev.html

peacefulrivers.homestead.com/Rumipoetry1.html

www.mikeshane.org/rumi

www.whirlingdervishes.org

en.wikipedia.org/wiki/Jalal_ad-Din_Muhammad_Rumi

www.rumisongs.com

www.rumi.net/rumi_poems_main.htm

www.farhangsara.com/jalal_al.htm

www.islamicamagazine.com/content/view/92/61/

www.drsoroush.com/lectures-english.htm

Appendix C

Glossary

Allah The name for God in the Arabic language. From the same linguistic root as the Hebrew word for God, El or Eloh. The whirling dervishes chant this holy name, among many other similar sayings, in their meditative rituals.

Chelebi (also *Celebi*) A noble person. Also the title given to Rumi's top student, Husamuddin. Rumi's descendants take this title as their family name. The worldwide head of the Rumi family also is known by this epithet as a title of respect.

dervish (also *darwish*) From the Persian word for doorway or threshold. This is a name used to describe a Muslim religious ascetic, someone who is at the doorway on his or her search for God.

diwan (also *divan*) A Persian term for a collection of poems, ruminations, or the discourses of an author.

fana A state of annihilation of the ego in union with God, in Sufi terms. Through meditation and self-denial, the Sufi seeks to merge his or her thoughts and being into the Divine wavelength. This concept is similar to the Buddhist state of nirvana.

hadith This means a saying or action spoken or performed by Prophet Muhammad. Rumi often alludes to these in his poetry.

khamush   A Persian word that means silence. Around 500 of Rumi's odes end with this word. He is emphasizing, in those instances, that silent contemplation is needed to absorb the lesson given.

mathnawi (also *Masnawi, Masnavi*)   A Persian term that refers to a type of poetry in which the two half verses of a couplet rhyme, and the rhyme keeps on changing from one verse to the next.

Maulana (also *molavi, mevlana, molvi*)   An Arabic title meaning a lord or master, usually of religious knowledge. It is pronounced *mevlana* in Turkish, *molvi* in Urdu, and *molavi* in Persian.

Mevlevi   The term by which the followers of Rumi are known.

muraqabah   The Sufi term for meditation, especially at night. It is derived from the Arabic word for "watching over something."

noor (*nūr*)   From the Arabic word for illuminated or light. Sufis use this term in conjunction with growing enlightenment and understanding.

Qur'an (also *Koran*)   The name of the Muslim holy book. Its literal meaning is, "that which is recited."

rubaiyat   From the Arabic word for the number four. It means a four-line quatrain, or group of rhymed verses.

Rum (also *Rūm*)   An Arabic designation meaning "of the Roman lands." Jalaluddin Rumi was known by this title because he had settled in Anatolia, a land recently won over by the Muslims from the Byzantine Romans.

sabr   An Arabic word that means patience and perseverance. This is a frequently cited quality that Sufis praise.

sama' (also *sema'*)   From the Arabic word "to hear." It is the act of opening oneself to listen to God, a state that Sufis seek to achieve when they meditate and chant. Some Sufi orders move in a rhythmic fashion as they chant during their *sama'* rituals. Others sit in large circular gatherings and chant in unison. The Mevlevi Sufis turn slowly in circles and achieve a trancelike state while reciting God's names. The basic principles of the generic Sufi *sama'* ritual originated in Baghdad several centuries before Rumi's time.

shaykh (also *sheikh*)   From the Arabic word for respected elder. This is the title given to a teacher or spiritual master among Sufis.

Sufi   From the Arabic word for wool. Early ascetics in the Muslim world wore coarse clothing to remind themselves of how temporary this life was. Thus, they achieved this nickname. A Sufi is a Muslim who is intensely interested in spiritual matters and wisdom and renounces all or part of his or her worldly life in the pursuit of God's pleasure.

sultan   An Arabic word that is synonymous with king or ruler.

tariqa   From the Arabic word *taa'ariq*, meaning a unique way or mode of doing things. This is the word used for a Sufi Order or Brotherhood. A typical *tariqa* has a leader, or *shaykh*, with various levels of disciples and acolytes under him (or her). It may have an international network.

tawbah   An Arabic word that means to seek repentance from God. This is an activity of great importance to Sufis who consider it an excellent way to combat any lurking sense of arrogance and also to bring themselves closer to God and His mercy.

tekke   A Turkish term for a building where Sufi brotherhoods hold their meetings. (This type of building is also known as a *khanqah* or *ribat*.) Oftentimes important leaders from that organization's past are buried in or around the *tekke*.

tenure   A cloak awarded to an initiate of the Mevlevi Sufi order after completing 1,001 days of compulsory service.

zikr (also *dhikr*)   From the Arabic word "to remember" or "to commemorate." This is a practice introduced by Muhammad of chanting God's names or attributes, especially after prayer. It is similar to the Catholic Rosary. Sufis emphasize this practice and use it as the basis for elaborate rituals.

Index

N-0

P

Check out these
BEST-SELLERS

READ BY MILLIONS!

Grammar and Style
SECOND EDITION

978-1-59257-115-4
$16.95

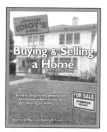
Buying & Selling a Home
FIFTH EDITION

978-1-59257-458-2
$19.95

FULL-COLOR!

The Perfect Wedding
Illustrated

978-1-59257-566-4
$22.95

Learning Spanish
FOURTH EDITION

978-1-59257-485-8
$24.95

Baby Sign Language

978-1-59257-469-8
$14.95

Total Nutrition
FOURTH EDITION

978-1-59257-439-1
$18.95

Positive Dog Training
SECOND EDITION

978-1-59257-483-4
$14.95

The Bible
THIRD EDITION

978-1-59257-389-9
$18.95

Music Theory
SECOND EDITION

978-1-59257-437-7
$19.95

The Perfect Resume
FOURTH EDITION

978-1-59257-463-6
$14.95

Playing the Guitar
SECOND EDITION

978-0-02864244-4
$21.95

Manga
ILLUSTRATED

978-1-59257-335-6
$19.95

Knitting & Crocheting
THIRD EDITION
Illustrated

978-1-59257-491-9
$19.95

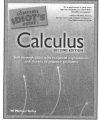
Calculus
SECOND EDITION

978-1-59257-471-1
$18.95

Investing
THIRD EDITION

978-1-59257-480-3
$19.95

More than **450 titles** available at booksellers and online retailers everywhere

ALPHA

www.idiotsguides.com

Great gifts for *any* occasion!

ISBN: 978-1-59257-645-6

ISBN: 978-1-59257-617-3

ISBN: 978-1-59257-599-2

ISBN: 978-1-59257-749-1

ISBN: 978-1-59257-557-2

ISBN: 978-1-59257-538-1

ISBN: 978-1-59257-631-9

ISBN: 978-1-59257-715-6

ISBN: 978-1-59257-567-1

ALPHA

idiotsguides.com